The Apple-Tree

by L. H. Bailey

I

WHERE THERE IS NO APPLE-TREE

The wind is snapping in the bamboos, knocking together the resonant canes and weaving the myriad flexile wreaths above them. The palm heads rustle with a brisk crinkling music. Great ferns stand in the edge of the forest, and giant arums cling their arms about the trunks of trees and rear their dim jacks-in-the-pulpit far in the branches; and in the greater distance I know that green parrots are flying in twos from tree to tree. The plant forms are strange and various, making mosaic of contrasting range of leaf-size and leaf-shape, palm and grass and fern, epiphyte and liana and clumpy mistletoe, of grace and clumsiness and even misproportion, a tall thick landscape all mingled into a symmetry of disorder that charms the attention and fascinates the eye.

It is a soft and delicious air wherein I sit. A torrid drowse is in the receding landscape. The people move leisurely, as befits the world where there is no preparation for frost and no urgent need of laborious apparel. There are tardy bullock-carts, unconscious donkeys, and men pushing vehicles. There are odd products and unaccustomed cakes and cookies on little stands by the roadside, where the turbaned vendor sits on the ground unconcernedly.

There are strange fruits in the carts, on the donkeys that move down the hillsides from distant plantations in the heart of the jungle, on the trees by winding road and thatched cottage, in the great crowded markets in the city. I recognize coconuts and mangoes, star-apples and custard-apples and cherimoyas, papayas, guavas, mamones, pomegranates, figs, christophines, and the varied range of citrus fruits. There are also great polished apples in the markets, coming from cooler regions, tied by their stems, good to look at but impossible to relish; and I understand how these people of the tropics think the apple an inferior fruit, so successfully do the poor varieties stop the desire for more. There are vegetables I have never seen before.

I am conscious of a slowly moving landscape with people and birds and beasts of burden and windy vegetation, of prospects in which there are no broad smooth farm fields with fences dividing them, of scenery full of herbage, in which every lineament and action incite me and stimulate my desire for more, of days that end suddenly in the blackness of night.

Yet, somehow, I look forward to the time when I may go to a more accustomed place. Either from long association with other scenes or because of some inexpressible deficiency in this tropic splendor, I am not satisfied even though I am exuberantly entertained. Something I miss. For weeks I wondered what single element I missed most. Out of the numberless associations of childhood and youth and eager manhood it is difficult to choose one that is missed more than another. Yet one day it came over me startlingly that I missed the apple-tree,--the apple-tree, the sheep, and the milch cattle!

The farm home with its commodious house, its greensward, its great barn and soft fields and distant woods, and the apple-tree by the wood-shed; the good home at the end of the village with its sward and shrubbery, and apple roof-tree; the orchard, well kept, trim and apple-green, yielding its wagon-loads of fruits; the old tree on the hillside, in the pasture where generations of men have come and gone and where houses have fallen to decay; the odor of the apples in the cellar in the cold winter night; the feasts around the fireside,--I think all these pictures conjure themselves in my mind to tantalize me of home.

And often in my wanderings I promise myself that when I reach home I shall see the apple-tree as I had never seen it before. Even its bark and its gnarly trunk will hold converse with me, and its first tiny leaves of the budding spring will herald me a welcome. Once again I shall be a youth with the apple-tree, but feeling more than the turbulent affection of transient youth can understand. Life does not seem regular and established when there is no apple-tree in the yard and about the buildings, no orchards blooming in the May and laden in the September, no baskets heaped with the crisp smooth fruits; without all these I am still a foreigner, sojourning in a strange land.

II

THE APPLE-TREE IN THE LANDSCAPE

The April sun is soft on the broad open fenced fields, waking them gently from the long deep sleep of winter. Little rills are running full. The grass is newly coolly green. Fresh sprouts are in the sod. By copse and highway the shad-bushes salute with their handkerchiefs. Apple-trees show tips of verdure. It is good to see the early greens of changing spring. It is good to look abroad on an apple-tree landscape.

As to its vegetation, the landscape is low and flat, not tall. There is a vast uniformity in plant forms, a subdued and constrained humility. A month later the leafage will be in glory, but that also will have an aspect of sameness and moderation. Perhaps the actual variety of species will be greater than in many parts of the abounding tropics, and to the careful observer the luxuriance will be as great, although not so big; but as I look abroad I am impressed with the economy of the prospect. It comes nearer to my powers of assimilation, quiets me with a deep satisfaction; the contrasts are subdued, the processes grade into each other imperceptibly in the land of the lingering twilight.

In this prospect are maples and elms and apple-trees. The maples and elms are of the fields and roadsides. The apple-trees are of human habitations and human labor; they cluster about the buildings, or stand guard at a gate; they are in plantations made by hands. As I see them again, I wonder whether any other plant is so characteristically a home-tree.

So is the apple-tree, even when full grown, within the reach of children. It can be climbed. Little swings are hung from the branches. Its shade is low and familiar. It bestows its fruit liberally to all alike.

The apple is a sturdy tree. Short of trunk and short of continuous limb, it is yet a stout and rugged object, the indirectness of its branching branches adding to its picturesque quality. It is a tree of good structure. Although its limbs eventually arch to the ground, if left to themselves, they yet have great strength. The angularity of the branching, the frequent forking, the big healing or hollow knots with rounding callus-lips, give the tree character. Anywhere it would be a marked tree, unlike any other.

The bark on the older surface sheds in short oblong irregular scales or plates that detach perhaps at both ends and often at the sides, clinging by the middle until the curl loosens them and they fall to the ground. These plates or chips are more or less rowed up and down the trunk and on the larger branches, yet the apple bark is not ridged and furrowed as on the elm. The bark is not checked in squares as on old pear-trees nor peeling as on cherries. In dry weather, the loose old bark is dark brown-gray, often supporting gray lichens, but in rain it is soft and nearly black, yielding pleasantly to the touch. In the forks, the bark is not so readily cast and there the chips may lie in heaps. On the young limbs and small trunks the bark is tight and close, not splitting into seams or furrows with the expansion of the cylinder but stretching and throwing off detached flakes and chips. Under the chips various insects hide or make some of their transformations. There the codlin-moth pupates. The old remains of scale insects may be found on the exterior. In the furrows about the dormant buds the eggs of plant-lice pass the winter.

To destroy these breeding and hiding places, many careful apple-growers scrape away the loose bark, being careful not to expose the quick living tissue; and on the younger wood the eggs of aphis and other pests, as well as cocoons and nymphs, are destroyed by vigorous winter spraying. The regular spraying of apple-trees, in the different seasons, more or less sterilizes the bark. Many forms of canker, due to fungi and bacteria, invade the bark, making sunken areas and scars, often so serious as to destroy the tree. All these features are discoverable in the apple-tree.

The trunk of the apple-tree is short and stout, usually not perfectly cylindrical and not prominently buttressed at the base. In old trees it is usually ribbed or ridged, sometimes tortuous with spiral-like grooves, often showing the bulge where the graft was set. The wood is fine-grained and of good color, and lends itself well to certain kinds of cabinet work and to the turning-lathe for household objects; it should be better known.

If left to itself, the tree branches near the ground, making many strong secondary scaffold trunks; but the plant does not habitually have more than one bole, even though it may branch from the very base; it is a real tree, even though small, and not a huge shrub. In the natural condition, the trunk often rises only a foot or two before it is lost in the branches; at other times it may be four or six feet high. Under cultivation, the lowest branches are usually removed when the tree begins to grow, and an evident clean trunk is produced. In Europe and the Eastern States, it has been the practice to trim the trunk clean to the height of four or six feet; but in hotter and drier regions the trunk is kept short to insure against sun-scald; and with the better tillage implements of the present day it may not be necessary to train the heads so high.

In old hill pastures, in many parts of the North, one sees curious umbrella forms and other shapes of apple-trees, due to browsing by cattle. A little tree gets a start in the pasture. When cattle are turned in, they browse the tender terminal growth. The plant spreads at the base, in a horizontal direction. With the repeated browsing on top, the tree becomes a dense conical mound. Eventually, the leader may get a strong headway, and grows beyond the reach of the browsers. As it rises out of grasp, it sends off its side shoots, forming a head. The cattle browse the under side of this head, as far as they are able to reach, causing the tree to assume a grotesque hour-glass shape, flat on the under part of the head, with a cone of green herbage at the ground. Sometimes pastures are full of little hummocks of trees that have not yet been able to overtop the grazers.

The winter apple-tree in the free is a reassuring object. It has none of the sleekness of many horticultural forms, nor the fragility of peaches, sour cherries and plums. It stands boldly against the sky, with its elbows at all angles and its scaly bark holding the snow. Against evergreens it shows its ruggedness specially well. It presents forms to attract the artist. Even when gnarly and broken, it does not convey an impression of decrepitude and decay but rather of a hardy old character bearing his burdens. In every winter landscape I look instinctively for the apple-tree.

We are so accustomed to the apple-tree as a part of an orchard, where it is trimmed into shape and its bolder irregularities controlled, that we do not think it has beauty when left to itself to grow as it will. An apple-tree that takes its own course, as does a pine-tree or an oak, is looked on as unkempt and unprofitable and as a sorry object in the landscape, advertizing the neglect of the owner. Yet if the apple-tree had never borne good fruit, we should plant it for its bloom and its picturesqueness as we plant a hawthorn or a locust-tree.

In winter and in summer, and in the months between, my apple-tree is a great fact. It is a character in the population of my scenery, standing for certain human emotions. The tree is a living thing, not merely a something that bears apples.

III

THE BUDS ON THE TWIGS

Now the buds begin to break. The firm winter-buds swell. Their scales part. Tips of green appear. Tiny leaves come forth, neatly rolled inward, growing as they expand, the stalks lengthening. Resurrection is astir in the tree.

Several leaves issue from every bud. From some buds arise only leaves; from others a flower-cluster emerges from the leaf-rosette, showing faint color even before it expands. Very close together and tight these unopened little flowers are packed as they emerge; if we had looked at them with a lens as they lay in the bud in the long winter we should understand why; now they escape their bonds and rapidly grow as they are delivered, yet at first pressed together by head and stem in their soft gray wool.

Thus are there two kinds of buds on the twig of the bearing apple-tree,--the leaf-buds (sending forth leaves only), and the flower-buds (bearing both leaves and flowers). And if we wish to analyze more closely, we discover two kinds of leaf-buds,--those that send forth a rapidly growing shoot bearing the leaves, and those from which the leaf-cluster remains practically sessile on the branch. These latter, or the strongest and best of them, will probably give rise to short fruiting spurs and the others to elongated leafy branches.

Before me as I write is an apple limb more than three feet long. It has been a vigorous grower, for it is only three years old. The years can be readily made out; there are two sets of "rings" separating them. You may see these rings on all young apple limbs. They represent the scars of the scales of the past terminal buds.

Three years ago my shoot was sent off from its parent branch; that year it grew but four inches, bearing leaves on its sides, in the axils of which developed buds for the winter and at the end a larger terminal bud. Let us call this shoot 1918. Two years ago (1919), whilst I was in a distant land, the terminal bud gave rise to a shoot nineteen inches long; two buds near the end of the 1918 shoot pushed out clusters of leaves and made spurs about one-half inch long; all the other buds, five in number, remained dormant, and now they are dead and are rapidly becoming mere scars. Last year (1920) the terminal bud of 1919 gave rise to a shoot fifteen inches long; three buds at the base of this two-year (1919) shoot remained dormant; fourteen buds produced spurs. It is now the spring of 1921; the 1920 shoot has four dormant buds at its base, ten rosettes of leaves from the other buds, and a pushing terminal shoot.

On my branch this year, therefore, are 5 plus 3 plus 4, or 12 dormant buds of all the years; 2 plus 14 plus 10, or 26 spurs; 1 terminal bud continuing the onward growth.

It is evident that the last two years were good ones for my apple limb, for the growths were long (19 and 15 inches) and most of the buds produced spurs. The result is evidenced also in the fact that the limb is this year laden with potential bloom. On 1918 the two spurs bear flowers, one of them only a single bloom and the other five blooms. On 1919 twelve of the fourteen spurs are bearing flowers in the following numbers: 5 flowers, 5, 5, 7, 5, 6, 5, 5, 5, 5, 5, 5 = 63 flowers. On 1920 are no spurs bearing flowers, but the terminal bud (as is frequent on vigorous young trees) bears five flowers. Here, therefore, on this yard of three-year-old twig are seventy-four blossoms.

But there will not be seventy-four fruits; some of the flowers are small and weak; others, as the petals fall, show unmistakable signs of failing. A few of them show the plump form of an embryo apple: I think there are a score of such promises. But I know that others will fail later from physiological causes, and others probably from onslaught of insects or disease or from accidents. If six fair fruits mature on a branch like this, the crop will be good; and probably the branch would not have vigor enough to set as many fruit-buds the following year or to bear as many fruits.

It is good to watch the opening of the apple bloom: pink buds swelling and puffing out each day, the woolly stems elongating, the five overlapping incurving petals spreading and growing big, the stamens, about twenty, straightening up and lengthening their filaments that are attached on the flower-rim; the big light yellow anthers shedding pollen; the five green styles in the center. In some flowers the styles do not develop, and we have one reason why many flowers are sterile.

The flower-clusters differ much among themselves, in size of parts, number of flowers, color; on some trees the flowers appear in advance of most of the leafage, but usually they are coincident with the leaves. Sometimes the flower-stems or peduncles are branched, bearing two or three flowers, and in that case there may be a small green leaf or bract where the fork arises. The placing of the petals in the bud at the epoch of expansion may differ in two flowers on the same tree. One petal may stand guard outside the others and free from them, both edges uncovered, while the remaining petals are spiral with one edge under and one edge over; or there may be two guard petals, one on either side; or sometimes all the petals may be spiral, one margin out, one margin in; in some cases all the petals stand free as the flower is expanding, with no margin interlapping. Sometimes one petal is missing, and again the petals may be six.

This infinite variety within the bonds of so great regularity lends a subtle charm to natural objects, that is wholly absent in man's perfected machine-work. Man aims at uniformity, two and two alike; nature aims at endless difference, every object or even every member of an object having its own character. Much of man's energy is expended in trying to overcome the diverseness of nature.

Gradually and slowly the flower balloons enlarge and puff themselves up, the petals standing together at their tips; all the variety is united into a harmony of exuberance, color and form; then one day there is a shower of genial rain, a warm sun, birds in the air, bees released, grasses soft and lush, and behold! the apple-tree is in bloom,--a great heavenly mound of white and pink exhaling a faint delicious breath. Then the pulses stir, the dogs bark at the edges of the wood, the fields call, the scented winds lead on forever.

IV

THE WEEKS BETWEEN THE FLOWER AND THE FRUIT

The petals expand broadly, usually losing most of their pink. The blade is oblong and rounded at the end, at first cupped and then nearly flat, three-fourths of an inch long, narrowed at the base into a short stem-like part and usually hairy there, the edges perhaps wavy but entire. The expanse of the flower may be one and one-half to two inches. The brush of stamens, erect in the center, sheds its pollen and the anthers collapse.

Then the petals fall, like flakes of snow, borne often by the wind. There remain the stout woolly flower-stems an inch or more long and bearing minute dry bracts, with the young fruit at the summit topped by the five recurving woolly sepals and the pencil of stamens and styles. The bloom being gone, the flowering system of the apple is thenceforth little observed. Not until the fruit begins to color do we come back to the apple-tree to look at it closely; yet in these intervening weeks some of the most interesting transformations take place, and on the exact observance of them depends to a large extent one's success in the rearing and saving of a good crop of apples.

Here is the flower of the apple-tree (Fig. 3). It is a comely blossom, fragrant and pinky white, flatly spread to the sky, carrying the spirit of the cool of the spring. What concerns us now, however, is the cluster of stamens and pistils in the center, for these organs are directly concerned in the production of the fruit. The petals soon fall, but the remains of these interior organs persist, even unto the ripening of the fruit.

The anther is attached at the back of its base or middle to the top of the filament in the suture separating the two large cells. These anther-cells split along the outer margins, releasing the pollen-grains.

In the center of the ring of stamens are the five style-branches, which are united at the base into a short hairy column; the column is borne on the ovary, which is sunken deep into the receptacle or stem (Fig. 4). It is down these style-branches that the pollen-tube passes on its way to the ovules or embryo seeds. The top of the style is expanded into a cupped stigma on which are many glutinous points. One can observe the browning and ripening of the stigma after pollen has been deposited by wind, bees or other agencies. When the ovules are fertilized, the forming fruit enlarges regularly unless it meets with misfortune or is crowded out for lack of room and nourishment.

If one cuts across the ovary or embryo fruit below the recurving sepals, one will see under a lens that it is neatly five-celled (Fig. 5). In each cell are two ovules; these, if all goes well, will ripen into ten seeds. These five cells comprise most of the diameter in the cross-section: but as the ovary enlarges and the young fruit grows, one may see that the inner part comprising the cells begins to have a character of its own and to be differentiated from the surrounding flesh.

[Illustration: 5. Cross-section of the ovary.]

The "blossom" falls. In reality only the petals fall. What is left is well shown in Fig. 6. Here remain the upstanding stamens with the empty anthers, and in the center one could see the five styles if the specimen were in hand. Here also are the calyx-lobes, widely spreading and even recurved. The photograph for Fig. 6 was taken May 3. On May 17 another cluster was photographed from the same tree (Fig. 7). Three of the flowers have produced sturdy young apples. The stems or pedicels have become stouter, and they begin to spread. Note that the calyx now is closed, the old stamens protruding, a circumstance that will have special significance when we become acquainted with the codlin-moth. Note also that one flower has failed, and remains as it was two weeks earlier; it will soon fall. The young apples begin to take shape. They show a glow of red on the cheek. They are fuzzy all over. One of them is already injured on one side, having been stung by a curculio or other insect: there are keen senses about the apple-tree.

Two weeks later (May 31) still another cluster was taken from the same tree (Fig. 8). Here are three fruits erect on their stems; one of them is more than an inch in diameter either way, sturdy and unblemished; another shows deformity due to insect puncture; the third remains small and presently will drop. A scar in the leaf-axil marks the failure of another flower. Four blossoms were in this cluster, but only one fruit now has a chance to come to uninjured maturity, and two have already failed. The big apple has now lost most of its fuzziness and begins to assume a delicate "bloom" on its surface; the smallest one--the one that soon will perish--still holds some of its fuzz. A section of this smallest fruit discloses empty cells; apparently it was not fertilized.

Another two weeks have passed. It is June 14th. From the same tree is taken the photograph, Fig. 9. Here is a big apple, 1-1/2 inch in diameter; and there is a dead shrivelled fruit that dropped when I touched it. Of the several flowers in the cluster, all have failed but one. This one fruit has now passed the danger of the blossom-end infection by the codlin-moth and it has no blemishes. The many whitish spots characteristic of the variety are now conspicuous all over the surface. The ribs begin to show. There is a faint blush on the upper side. The fuzz has disappeared and the bloom is becoming evident. The calyx is tightly closed, although the tips of the sepals are spread widely. The stem is stout. The weight of the apple inclines it nearly to the horizontal. Yet this good apple is not symmetrical; one side is larger than the other. I cut it crosswise and find two cells on the larger side developing two strong seeds each, whilst those on the smaller side have a single seed each and one of these seeds is small and perhaps would not have matured. The fleshy part of the apple, outside the core, now occupies about as much of the diameter as the core itself and much more than one-half the bulk of the fruit. Already my apple, now half grown, shows many of its distinctive characteristics.

Yet another fortnight has come and gone, and it is June 28th. It has been good "growing weather." Summer is here, full-orbed, regal, bringing the abundance of the earth. Here are two stout apples hanging on their stems (Fig. 10), for they are now too heavy to be held erect. The larger fruit is a trifle more than two inches in diameter. The feature spots are now still more prominent on these apples, the ribs more pronounced, the blush against the sun more warm. Both these fruits, from one spur, will mature; but the smaller one will be blemished, for the apple-scab fungus has established itself on the crown and about the calyx. Already the growth is checked in that area, and the apple looks flattened. There is no evidence in either apple of codlin-moth invasion. The adjoining spur, not clearly shown in the photograph, is barren; it gave no flowers this year, and it shows no indication of a blossom-bud for next year. The leaves are thick and vigorous, yet they bear marks of insect injury and one of them has been extensively skeletonized. On the whole, however, the fruits have the mastery, and they now make a brave show.

July has passed this way. Tomorrow it will be August. The odor of apples is now in my tree. There are big striped apples on the ground, plucked by the wind, the hold loosened by bugs for they too have felt the fullness of July. Three apples, one of them three inches through and two and one-half inches high, and the others nearly as big, hang at the level of my eyes. You may see them in Fig. 11. Here rises again my boyhood spent in an orchard now passed away, as father and mother have passed, as playmates have fallen one by one, the old place holding only memories. Here is my boyhood because the earth is always young and repeats her miracles for the children by my side as it did for me so many many years ago. Yet the miracles are greater now than they were then. They have more meaning. Now are they part of some great order.

They are not separate. Without moving my feet, I lay my hands on apples, Virginia creeper, asparagus, marigold, sweet sultan, oxalis, plantain, crab-grass, white clover, all growing securely in one place, and everyone like unto itself alone. Here is the everlasting miracle before my eyes, and all miracles are mysteries. Once I thought I should understand such things when I was "grown up," but I find myself still a boy.

These three apples on the last of the days of July look fair and sound, partly hidden in the leaves, the deep red colors covering them in broad splashed stripes and relieved by light dots. Yet when I raise the leaves or when I lift the apples apart, I find the burrows of insects. They know that these apples are good. It is astonishing how nature covers up the wounds, how she conceals the sore places, and how fair she makes everything look. Were it not that she covers the depredations of man, the earth would not long remain habitable by him.

Summer is ended. Today the sun is on the equator, and we are at the equinox when nights are equal to the days, as the word testifies. The harvest is over. The apples are no more. Yet the tree still is active and preparing for another year (Fig. 12). The spurs are now thick and stout, bearing sturdy hard leaves. The bud in the center is a big one, already recognized as a fruit-bud: here is the promise of speckled, furrowed, striped apples next August. Thereby I learn that it is not enough to be good to the tree in the year in which I desire its fruit: I must begin the year before, and the year before that, and even back at the time when the tree is planted; and if the tree at planting-time is not a good tree, it will be at a disadvantage perhaps all its life long.

Finally the apple is ripe and ready. At the stem end is the "cavity," a depression, deep or shallow, according to variety, in which the stem is set. At the blossom end is the "basin," also with the characteristics of the variety as to depth and width and contour, in which the calyx-lobes persist, and inside the calyx are the remains of the dead stamens and styles; the calyx may be "closed" or "open," the character being a mark of the particular variety.

Cut the apple through the center lengthwise (Fig. 13); note the curved outline of the core (the pistil) extending half or more across the fruit; if you do not see this outline, cut an apple until you do; carefully open the five cells or compartments and within the parchment walls find the two seeds attached by their points which are directed toward the stem end; perhaps one of the seeds has failed, but probably a cavity marks its place; perhaps both seeds have failed; perhaps the cell has more than two seeds.

Cut an apple cross-wise: note the five radiating cells of the core, the number and attachment of the seeds; note the ten points, imbedded in the flesh, marking the outline of the core. Cut an apple cross-wise above the core and beneath it; note where these points vanish and try to harmonize them with the core-outline as seen in the lengthwise section; probably you will discover why you may not see the core-outline in all the lengthwise sections you make. Before you leave the fruit, note whether single seeds in a cell are the same shape as the two seeds in a cell.

The flesh outside the core-outline is interpreted to be stem structure rather than pistil structure. Sometimes an apple bears a scale-like leaf on its exterior, suggesting that the outer part of the fruit is stem. The older morphologists interpreted the apple flower to comprise a hollowed calyx (calyx-tube) inside which is the pistil and on the rim of which are the petals and stamens. The structure now is regarded as a hollowed receptacle or stem (hypanthium), with the pistil inside, the petals and stamens on its rim. We noted in the flower that the ovary part of the pistil is solidly imbedded in this receptacle, but that the five styles are free. The pear and quince are of similar structure, but the peach, plum and cherry are simple ripened pistils.

Here, in this chapter, we have discovered some of the epochs in the life of the apple. Usually we let the imagination run only to the mature fruit, thinking of the harvest, but in all the weeks before the harvest the apple has been growing and taking form. As these weeks have not been blank to the apple-tree, so shall they not be blank to me.

V

THE BRUSH PILE

Today I visited the brush pile back of the orchard. Here the trimmings of the winter are placed, waiting to be burned when dry. How many are the archives that will be destroyed! Here are histories in every bud and twig and scar, of the seasons, of the accidents and deaths, the records of the tree as there are records of families.

These records are not written in numbers or in letters, nor yet in hieroglyphs; yet are they understandable. Alphabet is not needed, and the key is simple.

From the brush pile of records I took one. I must describe it in part by a picture (Fig. 14). On the living trees at this writing the petals mostly have fallen and the leaves are nearly full grown. This branch was cut in winter. It has lain in the snow and rain, putting forth no flowers or leaves. Yet we can read it.

It is May, 1921. The terminal shoot is obviously of 1920; we shall name it No. 1. It is a foot long, smooth and glossy, terminating at the base (o) in a "ring" and at a short stub or branchlet. If we count the buds on all sides of the shoot and at the tip we find them to be 13. The largest one is at the tip, and they are mostly successively smaller toward the base. Apparently the growth-energy was expended in the upper parts of the twig, making large full buds. In fact, the three or four lowermost buds are scarcely developed and would not grow unless the limb were broken off above them; they are dormant buds.

[Illustration: 14. A three-year record.--In a leisure hour, trace the history of these parts; it will open your eyes.]

Looking along the shoot, I find that every six buds stand in the same line: the sixth bud is over the first, seventh over the second, eighth over the third. If I were to fasten a string to bud No. 1 and wind it around the stem to my left, passing over every bud until I had reached the sixth, I should find that it had made two circuits of the stem (passed twice around it) and had passed over five spaces between buds. This is the leaf-arrangement or phyllotaxy of the apple-tree, expressed by the fraction 2/5. The space between two buds is two-fifths of a diameter, and two circuits (ten-fifths) must be passed before a bud comes over the one from which we started. The 2/5 leaf-arrangement obtains on cherry, peach, apricot, pear, raspberry and many others; but a very different order is that of the linden, grape, currant, lilies, elm, maple.

We cannot understand this simple unbranched terminal twig (No. 1) until we know what took place last year. A year ago, in the spring of 1920, a terminal bud that had formed in 1919 expanded and gave rise to this rapidly growing shoot. By the end of May or early June this shoot had grown to twelve inches long, for the growth in length on the twigs of trees is usually completed that early. This shoot bore leaves on the 2/5 arrangement; in the axil of every leaf was a bud, the strongest buds being with the strongest leaves at the middle and top of the shoot; in the autumn of 1920 these leaves fell, but the buds remained, persisted the winter, and were ready to "grow" in the early spring of 1921. We see them on No. 1 (Fig. 14).

[Illustration: 15. The growing shoot, with a bud in each axil, and a spur on last year's growth.]

In 1921 these buds on No. 1, then, would have grown. New leaves would have come from the bud itself; in fact, the winter buds of the apple are packed with miniature leaves and sometimes with flowers as well. The shoot coming out of the bud may remain very short, constituting a "spur," or grow with long internodes, making a slender twig. Fig. 15 shows a branch with new elongated growth, b to a, and a shoot or spur (c) arising from a bud of the previous year. Note the "ring," or division beyond b, marking the turn of the year.

It will be noted in Fig. 14 that the buds are of two shapes and sizes, such as a, a, a, representing one kind and b, b, the other kind. The former, small and pointed, are leaf-buds; from them will arise a shoot bearing only leaves. The latter, b, large and rounded and usually more fuzzy, are flower-buds (fruit-buds): from them will arise a short shoot bearing leaves and a cluster of flowers; and we hope that at least one of the flowers will set fruit.

We are now ready to resume our lesson with the branch before us. We have identified the slender terminal part, No. 1, as the growth of 1920. We are now to account for all the remaining buds and branchlets.

If No. 1 grew in 1920, then the main shoot of No. 2 grew in 1919, from the point o o. It is also one foot long. Near its base are four small buds that remained dormant in 1920. There are nine branches (d) of various lengths besides the terminal shoot No. 1, all of which grew in 1920, for they are naturally a year younger than the main axis from which they arise; these branches are the same age as No. 1, with buds that would have produced shoots in 1921. But the terminal buds of eight of these lateral shoots (all but the lowermost) bear blossom-buds at the end; note their size and shape. Had not the branch been cut, these buds would have bloomed in 1921; the eight of them would have produced probably forty to fifty flowers; perhaps two or three good fruits would have resulted. Note that two of the lateral branches or spurs are short and weak: these would soon perish. The No. 2 branch has a dead end (e); in some way the terminal bud was destroyed, and No. 1 sprang from a lateral bud beneath it, changing the direction of growth.

If No. 2 grew in 1919, then No. 3 grew in 1918. It also grew about one foot in length, showing that the conditions in the three years must have been very uniform. There are remains of five dormant buds at its base. There are seven side branches. As the main axis is three years old, so these lateral shoots are two years old; they are the same age as the axis No. 2. The lower one (s) grew less than an inch in 1919, and made a fruit-bud; in 1920 it blossomed and one fruit set as is shown by the square scar at the end; as the scar is small and the twig weak, we are safe in assuming that the apple was very small or else did not mature. A bud formed at the side of s to continue the growth of the spur next year (1921), but it is a leaf-bud; apparently there was not sufficient energy to bear flowers and to make a fruit-bud; so there would have been no more fruit on this spur earlier than 1922: thus do we see that the alternate bearing of the apple-tree may have some of its origin in the fruit-spur.

The side spur f produced a terminal blossom-bud in 1919. In 1920 six flowers opened,--I could count the scars. One of the flowers produced a fruit, as I tell by the square scar at the end; the thickened stem also indicates fruit-bearing. The side bud in this case is a fruit-bud, but it is small and weak and is probably incapable of producing a fruit. There are no strong leaf-buds to take up the work, and this spur (f) would probably soon have died, as also would spur s.

The side shoot g grew to h in 1919 and made a flower-bud. In 1920 this bud gave blossoms and one fruit resulted; the scar is prominent and there is an enlargement of the tissue indicating that the fruit probably attained good size; in 1920 also, two side spurs were formed each with weak blossom-buds, also a terminal shoot (beyond h) with leaf-bud at the end.

The other shoots have similar histories: the long shoot i bore a fruit-bud at k in 1919 and a fruit in 1920; in 1920 it also made three lateral shoots and a terminal shoot, with flower-buds terminating two of them. Shoot l bore flowers at its point in 1920 but did not carry the fruit to maturity; it also made two side growths and one terminal growth, all terminated by flower-buds, to be blown in 1921. The shoot m is a short spur that made a flower-bud in 1919 and in 1920 carried three little fruits for a time and made a flower-bud in 1920. Shoot n remained very short in 1919, making a terminal leaf-bud; in 1920 it grew two inches and made a weak flower-bud.

If shoot No. 3 grew in 1918, then No. 4 grew in 1917; but the branch is severed and I cannot trace the record farther. We could trace the family history many years if we had the unpruned tree before us.

Here, then, in my yard-long manuscript are forty bud-records on the main axis, counting the terminals on No. 2 and No. 3. I can find record of 144 buds on the side shoots. This makes a grand total of 184 buds. There is a total growth in length of 108 inches, or 9 feet. Each of the buds that has already "grown" has produced an average of probably ten leaves, or say 340 leaves in total. If there were an average of five flowers to the cluster, then about 150 flowers would have been carried on my branch, with the potentiality of 150 fruits; but in fact not more than three or four maturing fruits would have been produced in these years: and I should think this a good proportion as blossoms and apples go. Certainly the branch has done its part. There have been three eventful years.

I would not have my reader to suppose that one may always distinguish leaf-buds and fruit-buds at a glance. I may be mistaken in some of the above determinations, but they are essentially correct for I have the twig before me. In some varieties of apples the differences between the two kinds of buds are less marked. The certain way is to dissect the bud: one may then see what it contains.

It now remains to determine how the branch was placed in the tree. It must have been upright or very nearly so, for the main axis is essentially straight and the branchlets are about equally developed on all sides; moreover, there is no indication in the bark that one exposure was the "weather side." The big twig i apparently found a light and unoccupied space into which to develop, but its extension is not greatly out of proportion. I suppose, however, that my branch was not topmost in the tree; there is no indication in very long growth or strong upward tendency of the branchlets to mark the branch as a "leader."

Years ago I became fascinated with the study of knots and knot-holes in the timber of wood-piles. They are excellent records of the events in the life of trees. In print I have tried to show what they mean. I also worked out the life-histories of twigs and published them in nature-study leaflets and elsewhere. Hundreds of children were interested in the twigs and buds, finding them unusual, every one of them a different story, and yet not difficult to read. These lessons gave meaning to trees and seasons. Such observations have always meant much to me, even when made in the most casual way in the midst of constraining activities. And now in this later day I come back to a bare twig with all the joy of youth. The records of the years are in these piles of brush.

VI

THE PRUNING OF THE APPLE-TREE

We have found that not all the buds grow. We also know that some of the spurs and shoots perish, not alone from accident but from defeat in the struggle to live. The chances of success are relatively few. The pruning process begins early in the life of the tree, and it continues ceaselessly until the end.

To the apple-tree in the wild, strict pruning is the assurance of success. No tree can reach maturity unless more parts perish than are able to live. The young forest tree has branchlets and leaves along its side and at the top. All these perish as the trunk rises, often leaving marks on the bark, curls in the wood, and knot-holes large and small. Thousands of perished buds and branches are the price of a straight bole and great clear sheets of boards. Yet these perished parts bore their burden in their day and time, and contributed to the ultimate success: there could have been no tree without them.

Any tree-top discloses the pruning in action if one looks intently. Part of it is recorded in the buds that never put forth a leaf; more of it in little shoots left behind; and there are large and small limbs, dead and dying, yellowing apparently before their time, hanging on till the last hold is broken. Were it not for the benevolent processes of decay, the ground would be strewn with the fallen parts accumulating through the years.

In nature, the great result is to yield abundant quantity of seeds, that the species may propagate itself after its kind. Man may desire fruits relatively few, but large of size and excellent of quality, without spot or blemish; this means greater opportunity and care to the single fruit. Pruning is essential, to converge the energy of the plant into fewer branches, to give the fruits space and light, to increase the efficiency of measures for the control of diseases and insects. Part of the pruning consists in removing certain branches, and part of it in eliminating the fruits themselves by the careful process of thinning.

The pruning of nature is fortuitous. The tree has the irregularity and abandon of the picturesque. The pruning of man is for a different end, and it produces the comely well-proportioned tree of the orchards. The tree becomes a manipulated subject, comforting to the eye of the thrifty pomologist.

Branch-pruning is essentially the removal of superfluous branches,--those that crowd, that cross each other, that are so placed as to be profitless, that are in the way, that are injured or diseased. For the most part, the branches should be removed when they are small; but it is not possible to foresee all that may be needed in the training of the tree and, therefore, the frequent advice to prune only with a hand-knife cannot be followed. One needs a sharp pruning-saw and sometimes a chisel on a long handle. Usually it is not necessary to remove branches more than an inch or one and one-half inch in diameter if pruning is carefully practiced every year; but sometimes even well-pruned trees must be shaped, corrected and improved by the cutting of larger branches.

Pruning is usually best performed in early spring. The branch should be cut close to the main limb or trunk and parallel with it, leaving no stub; the healing process is then likely to proceed more rapidly. The wound should be smooth and clean, without breaks, splinters or splits; the knot-holes in logs and trunks are usually the consequence of long "stubs" and torn injured parts. The tree is to be left shapely, with a uniform distribution of branches, plenty of fruit-bearing wood, easy to spray and from which to pick the fruit, of the form characteristic of the variety.

In all the usual customary pruning of the apple-tree, dressing of the wounds is not necessary. It is much more important to give the added attention to the proper making of the wounds and the thoughtful choice of the parts to be removed. Wounds two inches and more in diameter may be protected with good paint, so that they will not check and therefore not hold water, until the callus covers them. Good judgment in pruning is more profitable than recipes to repair damage.

Fruit-pruning, or thinning, is the removing of so much fruit, when it is small, as will allow the remainder to mature to its best and constitute a maximum yield; it reduces the quantity of inferior fruit, lessens the number of culls and the labor at packing time, conserves the energy of the tree by preventing the maturity of great numbers of seeds, diminishes diseases and pests. The overloading of the tree not only imposes a heavy tax on its vitality but is likely to break the limbs and to work much physical damage.

Thinning may consist in removing part of the fruit in the cluster (in the case of varieties that tend to mature more than one fruit from each flower-cluster), in picking all the fruits from certain clusters or pairs of clusters, or in cutting away some of the fruit-spurs before blossoming time.

The removal of the fruit itself is usually performed after the "June-drop," when the extent of the crop is evident. The fruits are pulled off by hand or cut with thinning-shears, the latter practice being the better since it is not so likely to break the fruit-spurs. The least promising fruits are taken away and the remaining apples are left at least five or six inches apart in most varieties. The extent of thinning must be governed by the variety, thrift of the tree, result desired, and other conditions. To secure the best results, the apples should be thinned when still small.

Thinning by early-spring removal of fruit-spurs is a very special practice. It is employed on dwarf trees and on those specially trained. It should be undertaken only by a careful and experienced man. It is not to be inferred that the fruit of the apple is all borne on spurs, for some of it may be derived from terminal buds on the new axial growths or even from lateral buds; but the spurs are conspicuous and readily recognized. Of course the ordinary pruning of the tree removes fruit-bearing wood and is therefore a thinning process.

Within sensible limits, therefore, pruning is an invigorating process in the sense that it deflects the energy to remaining parts of the tree. What is called too heavy pruning, whereby the tree throws out abundance of water-sprouts, is illustration of this fact: the tree is thrown into heavy growth of adventitious shoots. The tree may not produce more pounds of substance, or even more total feet in length, but new energy is developed in certain parts.

In the restoration, or so-called renovation, of old neglected trees, the two primary considerations are to prune vigorously and to till and fertilize the land. Sometimes old trees must be mended as explained in

Chapter XIII.

Of course they must be sprayed for what ails them. If the variety is poor, the tree may be top-grafted (Chapter XII). In some cases, it is hardly possible to make neglected trees bear satisfactorily, for they were never of value: there is nothing to restore. It may be a question of soil and location, of lack of pollination, of trees so weak or so misshapen that effort on them is wasted. But tillage, pruning, spraying, should produce worth-while results in most cases.

In the care of the fruit-tree there is no practice which brings the grower into such intimate knowledge of the plant as that of pruning and thinning. The operator sees the tree as a whole, taking it all in; then he sees it in small detail in all its parts, even to the spurs and buds. With simple good tools, sharp and keen, and with a practiced eye, he applies a deft and swift handicraft, cutting true, making a fair clean wound, leaving the tree comely and ready for its highest effort. The pride of good workmanship may find expression. The operator feels also the sense of mastery that is in him, whereby he corrects the tree, removes the wayward parts, keeps and encourages all that is best. To engage in this kind of education requires that one approaches the work with due preparation of mind and I think also with consecration of heart.

VII

MAINTAINING THE HEALTH AND ENERGY OF THE APPLE-TREE

The apple-tree starts life fresh and vigorous. It grows rapidly. The shoots are long and straight. The wood is smooth and fair and supple. The leaves are usually large. It is good to see the young trees acquire size and take shape.

Room in the ground and in the air is ample with the young apple-tree. It is free to grow. Probably the ground was newly prepared and tilled when the tree was planted; at least, a hole was dug and fine good earth was placed about the roots. Probably insects had not found permanent encampment on the tree. It had been well pruned, so that it carried the minimum of superfluous and competing parts.

But in time the difficulties come. The tree probably slows down. It becomes too thick of branches. The land is not tilled. It is not manured. Insects and fungi make headway. The tree overbears. As the years go on, the tree is thrown into alternate bearing, one year a crop too heavy, one year a crop too light. The tree becomes broken, diseased, gnarly, unshapely.

We have seen that the fruit-spur in bearing is likely to make a leaf-bud for the next year's activities rather than a flower-bud. It is assumed that the making of a flower-bud requires more energy than the making of a plain leaf-bud; if this is true, there may not be energy enough to carry a flower-cluster and to make a new flower-bud at the same time. But if the tree is in proper vigor, is well fed, protected from noxious organisms, not allowed to overbear, it should have sufficient energy to make a crop every year, frosts and accidents excepted. It is assumed, of course, that self-sterile varieties have good pollinizing varieties near them; it is always well to plant two or more kinds near together. Whether the continuity of bearing is exhibited on the same fruit-spurs or whether there may be an alternation in the spurs on the same tree, is of no moment in this discussion. It is enough to say that there is no reason in the nature of the case why an apple-tree should bear only every other year; it is probably a question of nutrition.

The first essential to continued health and vigor is to start with a strong unblemished tree. It is to be planted before its vitality is lessened by exposure and hard usage. The more direct the transfer from nursery to orchard, the better. It is to be placed in good ground, well drained and deeply spaded or plowed. The apple-tree thrives on many kinds of land, but light sand, hard clay, and muck are equally to be avoided. "Good corn land" is commonly considered to be good apple land. Certain soils and regions are particularly adaptable to commercial apple-growing, but the amateur may plant quite independently of this fact. The observant man notes the many conditions under which the apple-tree may be grown with satisfaction.

If the land is not uniformly prepared, then the hole dug for the tree should be larger than demanded by spread of roots, and the earth fined in the bottom of it. Trees should be planted when perfectly dormant, preferably in spring, at least in the northern parts.

The roots should be cut back to sound unsplintered wood, and very long roots may well be shortened. The reader is aware that roots have no regular order or arrangement as do the buds from which branches arise. It is not necessary to try to shape the root-system to any formal regularity.

As a good part of the root-system is destroyed when the tree is dug, so is the top reduced to insure something like a balance. Half or more of the top, on a three-year-old tree, is cut away, the long growths being shortened to perhaps three or four good buds. If limbs are left to form the framework of the future top, they should be alternate with each other at some distance apart so that weak crotches do not form.

The tree is planted snugly, the earth being filled among the roots so that no air-holes remain. The tree is shaken up and down to settle the earth densely. Once or twice in filling, the earth is packed with the feet. The purpose is to keep the tree firm and stiff against winds, and to give all its roots close contact with the earth. Properly planted, so that it will not whip or dry out, the tree gets a hold quickly and begins to grow strongly. The first start-off of the tree is important.

Apple-trees are held in vigor by plenty of room. For the standard varieties in regular orchards, the recommended distance either way is 40 feet, or 35 x 40 feet. Some varieties may go as close as 30 feet; and in regions (as parts of central and western North America) in which the trees are not expected to attain such great size as in the eastern country, the planting may be even less than this of the upright-growing kinds. The spaces between the trees may be utilized for a few years with other crops, even with other fruits, as peaches or berries. Orchardists sometimes plant smaller-growing and early-bearing varieties of apples between the regular trees as "fillers," taking them out as the room is needed. Of course all kinds of double cropping require that extra attention be given to the tilling and fertilizing of the plantation.

The general advice for the growing of strong apple-trees is to give the land good tillage from the first and to withhold other cropping after the trees come into profitable bearing. Clean tillage for the first part of the season and the raising of a cover-crop in the latter part, to be plowed under, is a standard and dependable procedure. Trees live long in continuous sod and they may thrive, but they may be expected to show gains under tillage. Vast areas of apple plantings are in sod, but this of itself does not demonstrate the desirability of the sod practice. Allowing trees to remain in sod usually leads to neglect.

There is a modification of sod-practice in some parts of the country that gives excellent results, under certain conditions. The grass is cut and allowed to lie, not being removed for hay. Manure and fertilizer are added as top-dressing, as needed. This method is known as the "sod mulch system." It is not a practice of partial neglect, like the prevailing sod orchards, but a regular designed method of producing results. Its application can hardly be as widespread as clean tillage, on level lands.

It is a common opinion that hillsides and more or less inaccessible slopes should be planted to apples. This may be true in the sense that apples will grow on such areas and that such plantations are better than fallow land. In fact, many such lands are profitable in orchards. When they do not allow of tillage, easy spraying, and economy in harvesting, however, they cannot compete with level orchards.

To maintain the health and energy of the apple-tree, the land should be enriched. This may be accomplished by the application of animal manures, chemical fertilizers, or cover-crops, or preferably by a combination of these means. Not many persons possess sufficient farm manures to supply the general crops and the apple-orchard; but every application the orchard receives is all to the good. Five to ten tons of good stable manure to the acre annually is a good addition for an orchard in bearing. This may be supplemented by cover-crops and bag fertilizers in years in which the manure is not available. Experiments are yet inconclusive on the fertilizing of apple-trees, but it is fair to assume that on most lands, particularly on old lands, the addition of chemical fertilizer is advantageous. A bearing apple-tree may receive two to eight pounds of nitrate of soda (depending on its size and on soil) applied to the full feeding area of the roots, five to nine pounds of acid phosphate, two or three pounds of muriate of potash; always ask advice.

The pasturing of orchards is often defensible and sometimes even desirable. If the trees are growing too rapidly, they may be "slowed down" by seeding to grass for a time; and pasturing with hogs, and possibly with sheep, may afford a way of keeping the area in condition and of adding fertilizer. Sheep that do not have access to drinking-water and salt gnaw the trees. Hogs root up the ground and thereby provide a rude kind of tillage. If animals are fed other food in the orchard, the fertilizer increment will be considerable.

In house-lot conditions, the apple-tree usually receives sufficient food if the land is well enriched for garden purposes; but trees in sod should have liberal top-dressings of fertilizer every year and of stable manure every other year.

The apple-tree should have a good supply of moisture. Planted on banks and in hard places about buildings, it may suffer in this respect. The land should be so graded that the rainfall will not run off. In orchard conditions, the moisture is conserved by the addition of humus to the land, and by thorough judicious tillage; and in dry regions it is supplied by irrigation.

The energy of the apple-tree, and its ability to produce, is conserved by holding all diseases and noxious insects in check. The means at the command of the apple-grower are now many. No longer is the man helpless, nor does he need to appeal to the moon or to "atmospheric influences" for reasons. The natural histories of fungi and insects, that do so much damage, are now a part of common understandable knowledge. To acquire at least a working understanding of the commonest of these subjects is in itself a great satisfaction and gives one a sense of dominion. The good books and bulletins are sufficient to keep one well informed. All these organisms are tenants of the apple-tree, and from the naturist's point of view alone they are not to be overlooked.

It is not to be inferred that all apple-trees will yield equally well with equally good treatment. There is difference in trees as there is in cows. We may not know why. But even so, it is our part to do the best we can: this is our privilege.

The tillage and care of plants lessen the struggle for existence. So is the apple-tree protected from the crowds, from contest for moisture and food, from insects, and from the competition within itself. Thereby is it able to express all its possibilities. Even the dormant potentialities may be wakened, and the plant makes a wide departure from its native state. This is not an original state of sin, but a state of repression in which it is held in a world that is full of so many things beside apple-trees. I may till my orchard ever so well, manipulate the trees ever so promptly, yet if the plantation then is allowed to run to neglect the processes of depreciation gain the mastery; the struggle for existence is restored.

To keep one's apple-tree in the pink of perfection is as joyful an enterprise as to do anything else well. It is only the well-conditioned tree that yields its glorious harvest year by year.

VIII

HOW AN APPLE-TREE IS MADE

If the seeds of a Baldwin or Winesap apple are planted, we do not expect to get a Baldwin or Winesap; we shall probably raise a very inferior fruit. The apple has not been bred "true to seed" as has the cabbage and sweet pea. To get the tree "true to name," of the desired variety and with no chance of failure (barring accident), is one of the niceties of horticulture. This is accomplished with great precision and despatch.

The apple-tree is started from the seed. It cannot be grown freely by means of cuttings, as can the grape and currant. In commercial practice the seeds are collected mostly from cider mills or from pomace. The seeds may be washed from the pomace, allowed to dry, and then mixed in sand, charcoal, sawdust or other material to prevent dessication and kept until spring, when they are sown. Or, if the land is not so wet in winter that the seed will drown or be washed out, the seed in the pomace (not separated) may be sown in autumn. The seeds are sown in drills, after the manner of onions or turnips, one to two or even three inches deep. They germinate readily in the cool of spring, and the plants should reach a height of twelve inches and more the first year.

If these plants were grown directly into bearing trees, it is probable that no two trees would produce the same kind of fruit. Some of the fruit might be summer apples, some of it winter apples, some red, yellow or striped, some of it flat, oblong or spherical, most of it sour but perhaps some of it sweet. Probably every kind would be inferior to the parent stock or to standard varieties, although there is a fair chance that a superior kind might originate from a field of such plants.

Therefore, it is not the variety (that is, the top) that is wanted in the raising of these numerous plants, but merely the roots, on which desired varieties may be grown by the clever art of graftage. Yet not even all the roots may be wanted, for the growing plants may differ or vary in their stature and vigor as well as in their fruit. The discriminating grower, therefore, discards the weak and puny treelings at the digging time; or if the weak plants seem still to have promise, they may be allowed to grow another year before they are dug for the grafting.

This digging time is the autumn of the first year, when the plants have grown one season. They are then to be used as "stocks" on which to graft Baldwin, Winesap or other varieties. The growing of these apple stocks is a business by itself. Formerly, most of the stocks used in North America were imported from France, where special skill has been developed in the growing of them and where the requisite labor is available. But now the stocks are grown also in deep rich bottom lands of the Middle West, as in Kansas, where, in the long seasons, a large growth may be attained.

The methods of graftage of the commercial apple-tree are two--by cion-grafting whereby a bit of wood with two or three buds is inserted on the stock, by bud-grafting (budding) whereby a single bud with a bit of bark attached is inserted under the bark of the stock.

Cion-grafting is practiced in winter under cover. The stock is cut off at the crown and the cion spliced on it, or the root may be cut in two or more pieces and each piece receive a cion. The union is made by the whip-graft method (Fig. 16). The cion is tied securely, to keep it in place. The piece-root method is allowable only when the root is long and strong, so that a well-rooted plant results the first year. The cion is a cutting of the last year's growth (as of No. 1, in Fig. 14). However accomplished, the process is to supply the cion with roots; it is planted in another plant instead of in the ground.

The cion-grafts are now planted in the nursery row in spring. The cion starts growth rapidly, only one shoot being allowed to remain; this shoot forms the trunk or bole of the future tree. At the end of the first season, the little tree is said to be one year old, although the root is at least two years old; at the end of the second year it is two years old; the tree is sometimes sold as a two-year-old, but usually a year later as a three-year-old having a four-year-old root. In fact, however, the root and top may be considered, in a way, to be of the same age, particularly if only a piece of the root is employed, for the cion grew on its parent tree the same year the root was growing in the nursery.

The tree grew from the seed but it is no longer a "seedling" or a "natural;" it is now a grafted tree, destined to produce a named recognized variety of apple, maybe York Imperial, maybe Jonathan. We find seedling trees in old fields, in fence-rows, and in woods. These have grown from scattered seeds and have come to fruit without the arts of the propagator. They bear their own tops or heads, rather than the heads that a thrifty horticulturist would have put on them. Now and then such a tree produces superior fruit; then a discriminating pomologist discovers it, names it a new variety, and propagates it as other varieties are propagated. Thus have most of the prized varieties originated, without knowledge on the part of man of the ultimate processes. But now with the accumulating knowledge of the plant-breeder we hope to be able to foresee and probably to produce varieties of given qualities.

[Illustration: 17. A "bud" before tying.]

Bud-grafting is practiced in summer. The young trees, obtained from the grower of apple stocks, are planted regularly in nursery rows in spring, the top having been cut back to the crown so that a strong vigorous shoot will arise. In July and August or September, when this shoot is the size of a lead pencil and larger and the bark will peel (or separate from the wood), a single bud is inserted near the ground (Fig. 17). This bud is deftly cut from the current year's growth of the desired variety; it grows in the axil of a leaf (Fig. 15). The leaf is removed but a small part of the stalk or petiole is retained with the bud to serve as a handle. A boat-shaped or shield-shaped piece of bark is removed with the bud. This piece, known technically as a "bud," is inserted in an incision on the stock, so that it slips underneath the bark and next the wood, with only the bud itself showing in the slit; it is then tied in place.

The stock on which the bud is inserted has a two-year root, and the root is entire. For this reason, budded trees are usually very large and strong for their age when compared with piece-root trees grown under similar conditions of climate, tillage and soil.

The bud does not grow the year it is inserted in the stock; it is dormant until the following spring, as it would have been had it remained on its parent branch; but soon after it is inserted it attaches itself fast to the stock: it is a bud implanted from one twig to another. The following spring, if the operation is successful, the bud "grows," sending up a strong shoot that makes the trunk of the future tree. The top of the stock is cut away; in the merchantable tree, the bend or place may be seen where the stock and cion meet.

As in the case of cion-grafting, we now have a top of a known variety growing on the root of an unknown kind. The tree is sold at two or three years, counting the age of the top; and of course the tree is no longer called a seedling, and it produces its implanted variety as accurately as does the cion-grafted tree. Equally good trees are produced by both cion-grafting and bud-grafting.

The apple-tree is now "propagated," and is ready for the planting. Great hopes will be built on it, and the tree will probably do its part to justify them. Nobody knows how a bud from a Baldwin tree holds the memory of a Baldwin or from a Winesap tree the memory of a Winesap. Neither does anyone know why of two seeds that look alike one will unerringly produce a cabbage and the other a cauliflower. So accustomed are we to these results that we never challenge a twig of apple or a seed of cabbage: we assume that the twig or the seed "knows." Nor have we yet approached this question in our elaborate studies of plant-breeding. Here is one of the mysteries that baffles the skill of the physiologist and chemist, yet it is a mystery so very common that we know it not, albeit the life on the planet would otherwise be utter confusion.

IX

THE DWARF APPLE-TREE

We have learned that many kinds of apples and apple-trees may come from a batch of seeds. Differences are expressed in the tree as well as in the fruit. In fact, stature is usually one of the characteristics of the variety. Here I open Downing's great book, "The Fruits and Fruit-Trees of America," and find the description of a certain variety beginning: "Tree while young very slow in its growth, but makes a compact well-formed head in the orchard," and another: "Tree vigorous, upright spreading, and productive." We know the small stature and early bearing of the Wagener (wherefore it is often planted in the orchard as a filler), and the great wide-spreading head of the Tompkins King with the apples scattered through the tree.

Now it so happens that in the course of time certain great races of the apple-tree have arisen, we do not know just why or how. There is the race or family of the russets and of the Fameuse. So are there several races very small in stature, remaining perhaps no larger than bushes. If we were to propagate any of the ordinary apples on such diminutive stocks, we should have a "dwarf apple-tree."

The dwarf apple, then, is not a question of variety but of stock. Any variety may be grown as a dwarf by grafting it on a plant that naturally remains small, although some varieties are more adaptable than others to the purpose.

If seeds of the natural diminutive apple-tree are sown, a variety of trees and apples may be expected. The fruits would probably be inferior. Probably the stature would vary between different seedlings. If we are to get the effect of dwarfness, we must be sure that the stock is itself really dwarf. Therefore, to eliminate variation and also because seeds of natural dwarf apples may not be had in sufficient quantity, the stocks are propagated by layers rather than by seeds.

The diminutive tree, when well established, is cut off near the ground. Sprouts arise. Some kinds sucker very freely. If earth is mounded up around the sprouts, roots form on them and the sprouts may be removed and treated as if they were seedling stocks. Usually the mounding is not performed until the shoots have made one season's growth. Gooseberries and some other plants are often propagated by mound-layers. In the case of the gooseberry, however, it is desired that the layer reproduce the parent--it may be Downing or Whitesmith--and therefore it is planted without further manipulation. But in the case of the apple, we do not want the layer to reproduce the parent, for the parent would probably bear an inferior fruit since it does not represent an "improved" or recognized variety; therefore the layer is grafted or budded with the particular variety we desire to grow as a dwarf tree.

Dwarf trees are grown in America, if at all, only in gardens, where extra attention may be given them. Only high-class kinds should be attempted on dwarfs, for the quantity-production of commercial apples must be obtained by less intensive methods on cheaper lands.

Better fruits often are grown on dwarf than on standards, for two reasons: It is usual to propagate only the best varieties on dwarf stock; the little tree must receive extra care in pruning and in every other way. Its bushel of apples must be choice, every one, to make the effort of growing the tree worth the while. Under European conditions where land is high-priced and labor has been relatively cheap, it is possible (and common) to raise apples on dwarfs for market, as it is profitable to terrace the hillsides with human labor; but in North America the conditions are practically the reverse and the dwarf tree cannot compete with the standard orchard tree.

The growing of a dwarf tree is essentially a gardening practice. It requires great skill. The spurs are produced and protected to a nicety. Every fruit may be the separate product of handwork. The fertilizing, mulching, watering, are carefully regulated for every tree. Often the trees are trained on cordons, espaliers, trellises or walls. The individual fruits may be tied up or bagged. All this is very different from the raising of apples by means of tractors and other machinery, gangs of pruners and pickers, broadside extensive methods, with highly organized systems of handling and marketing, in all of which the money-measure is the chief consideration. It is for all these reasons that the growing of a few dwarf apple-trees may afford such intimate satisfaction to a careful man who prizes the result of his skill.

The dwarfs are grown as little trees branching near the ground, headed in at top and side and kept within shape and bounds. If they are of the dwarfest dwarfs and not trained on trellis or wall (as they usually are not in America), the fruit may be gathered by a man standing on the ground, even from old trees. The dwarfs are planted eight to ten feet apart when grown in regular plantation.

Be it said that certain kinds of stocks produce trees only semi-dwarf; and in all cases if the tree is planted so deep that roots strike from the cion, the top will probably outgrow the stock, being supplied in part or even entirely by its own roots.

This brings us to a consideration of some of the kinds of dwarf stocks, or dwarf races of the apple-tree. Be it said, in understanding of the subject, that there are naturally dwarf forms of many plants, and probably all ordinary plants are capable of producing them. Thus there are very compact condensed forms of arbor-vitae, Norway spruce, peach-tree. These have originated as seed sports and are multiplied by cuttings. So are there dwarf tomatoes, dwarf China asters, dwarf sweet peas, all coming more or less true from seeds, for these species (of short generations) have been bred to reproduce their variations. The inquirer must not suppose, therefore, that the races of dwarf apple-trees are an anomaly in the vegetable kingdom.

It is customary to speak of two classes or races of dwarf apple-trees, the Paradise and the Doucin. The former kinds are the smaller, the trees on their own roots sometimes reaching not more than four feet in height at full bearing maturity. On the Paradise stocks, the grafted apple-tree is very small; it is a true dwarf. The Doucin trees are by nature larger, and apples grafted on them make semi-dwarf trees, midway in stature between the real dwarfs and the common standard or "free" apple-trees.

The case is not so simple, however, as this brief statement would make it appear. There are many kinds of Paradise stock, as also of Doucin. If one were to bring together living plants of all the kinds of natural dwarfs and semi-dwarfs that could be found in nurseries and growing collections, one would undoubtedly find a nearly complete series, so far as stature of tree is concerned, from the very dwarf to the full-sized standard tree. To say that a person is growing grafted dwarf apple-trees does not signify how large the trees may be expected to grow, for one may not know the particular kind of stocks on which the variety is grafted. In fact, it is considered even in Europe, where dwarf apples are chiefly grown, that the proper identification of dwarf stocks is still a subject for careful investigation.

When the Paradise dwarfs first came into existence is undetermined. They appear to have been known in the Middle Ages. The many races, as the Dutch, French, Metz, Nonsuch, Broad-leaved, indicate an ancient origin. We cannot be too certain what apple-trees were meant in the early references to the Paradise apple. The fruits of the present natural Paradise apple-trees are not sufficiently attractive to justify us in considering them the "Tree of Paradise" or apple of the Garden of Eden, which circumstance is supposed by some to account for the name. "Paradise" was originally a park or pleasure ground, applied also to the Garden of Eden, and later to horticultural gardens. John Parkinson wrote his great treatise on horticulture, 1629, under the title, "Paradisi in Sole Paradisus terrestris; or, a Choice Garden of all Sorts of Rarest Flowers, etc." Now we use the word for gardens of bliss.

The word Doucin, from the Italian, is supposed originally to have designated apples of sweet flavor, but it now applies technically to a class or race of semi-dwarf apple-trees.

For the purpose of this little book, however, the interest in the dwarf apple centers not so much in the origin of the stock as in the natural-history of the tree itself and the good skill of hand and heart that one may expend in the growing of it. If one would come close to a plant, knowing it intimately in every season, causing it to respond to sympathetic treatment through a series of years, then a garden collection of dwarf apples may satisfy the desire. It is too bad that we do not have time to cultivate the dwarfs often in the yards and gardens of North America. We are more familiar with the raising of dwarf pears (which are grafted on quince stocks since there is no similar race of natural dwarf pear-tree), but we do not give them the thumb-

and-finger care that is demanded for the choicest results. The abundance of apples in the market should only stimulate the desire of the connoisseur to have trees and fruits that are wholly personal. The market produce can never gratify the affections.

X

WHENCE COMES THE APPLE-TREE?

If the dwarf apple-tree goes back to the Middle Ages and perhaps farther, then whence comes the apple originally? No one can surely answer. Carbonized apples are found in the remains of the prehistoric lake dwellings of Switzerland. When recorded history begins, apples were well known and widely distributed. The apple-tree is wild in many parts of Europe, but it is difficult to determine whether, in a given region, it is indigenous or has run wild from cultivation. Wild apple-trees are common in North America, but no one supposes that the orchard apple is native here.

Expert opinion generally considers that the apple is native in the region of the Caspian Sea and probably in southeastern Europe. Perhaps it had spread westward before the Aryan migrations. It had also probably spread eastward, but it is not a cultivated fruit in China and Japan except apparently as introduced in recent time. The apple is essentially a fruit of central and northern Europe, and of European migration and settlement.

It is a fertile retrospect to conceive of the apple as an attendant of the course of Western civilization. Without voice and leaving no record, it has nevertheless followed man in his wanderings, encouraged his attainment of permanent habitations, succored him in his emergencies. What the apple has contributed to sustenance can never be known, but we are aware that it yields its fruit abundantly, that it thrives in widely unlike regions and conditions, that the tree has the ruggedness to endure severe climates and to provide food that can be stored and transported. In the ages it must have stood guard at many a rude camp and fireside. It would be fascinating to know what the apple-tree has witnessed.

These early apples must have been very crude fruits measured by the produce of the present day. But other food was crude and man was crude. The North American Indians found the apple to be worth their effort; remains of some of the so-called Indian orchards of the Five Nations in New York persisted until the present generation. These were seedling apple-trees, grown from the stocks introduced by the white man. The French missionaries are said to have carried the apple far into the interior, and early settlers took seeds with them. The legends and records of Johnny Appleseed, sowing the seeds as he went, are still familiar. My father, like other pioneers, took seeds from the old New England trees into the wilderness of the West; the resulting trees were top-grafted, some of them as late as my time; I can remember the apples some of these seedling trees bore, the like of which I have never seen again, probably poor apples if we had them in this day but to a boy at the edge of the forest the very essence of goodness. As early as 1639, apples had been picked from trees planted on Governor's Island in Boston harbor. Governor John Endicott of Massachusetts Colony had an apple-tree nursery in the early day; in 1644 he says that five hundred of his trees were destroyed by fire. So the apple came early to be a standby on the new continent.

The apples of the colonists were not all for eating, but for drinking. The butts and barrels of cider put in cellars in the early times seem to us most surprising. Herein are suggestions of old social customs that might lead us into interesting historical excursions. The oldest book I possess on the apple is "Vinetum Britannicum: or, a Treatise of Cider," published in London in 1676; it treats also of other beverages made from fruits and of "the newly-invented ingenio or mill, for the more expeditious and better making of cider." The gradual change in customs, whereby the eating of the apple (rather than the drinking of it) has come to be paramount, is a significant development; the use of apple-juice may now proceed on another basis, on the principle of preservation and pasteurization rather than of fermentation.

It is the custom to call the apple Pyrus Malus. This is the name given by the great Linnaeus, with whom the modern accurate naming of plants and animals begins. The nomenclature of plants starts with his "Species Plantarum," 1753. Pyrus is the genus or group comprising the pears and apples, and Linnaeus included the quince; Malus is Latin for the apple-tree. Together the names represent genus and species,--the malus Pyrus.

These statements are easy enough to make, but it is impossible to demonstrate whether the common pomological apples are derived from one original species or from two or more. Many technical botanical names have been given in the group, but we need not pause with them here. It is enough for our purpose to know that the natural-history of the apple, as of anything else that runs to time immemorial, passes at the end into obscurity. We seem never to reach the ultimate origins or to find an end to our quests.

There are other apples than the common pomological orchard types. There are the crabs. In general usage, the word "crab" designates an apple that is small, sour and crabbed. Such apples are wildings or seedlings. They are merely depreciated forms of Pyrus Malus, and probably much like the first apples known to man. What are known to horticulturists as crab-apples, however, are other species of Pyrus, of different character and origin. We need not pause with the discussion of them, except to say that the commonest kinds are the little long-stemmed fruits of Pyrus baccata (berry Pyrus), native in eastern Europe and Siberia. These are the "Siberian crabs." The leaves and twigs are smooth, and the calyx falls away from the fruit, leaving a bare blossom end. These little hard handsome fruits are used in the making of conserves. Certain larger crab-apples, in which the blossom end is not clean or bare, as the Transcendent and Hyslop, are probably hybrids between the true crabs and the common apple; this class provides the main crab-apples of the markets.

When the settlers came to the country west and south of New England, they found another kind of crab-apples in the woods, truly native. The fruits were hard and sour, but they could be buried to ripen. The trees are much like a thorn-apple,--low, spreading, twiggy, thorny; but the pink-white large fragrant flowers are very different. The wild crab-apple was called Pyrus coronaria by Linnaeus, the "garland Pyrus." On the prairies is another species, Pyrus ioensis; it yields a charming double-flowered form, "Bechtel's crab." In the South are other species. In fact, P. coronaria itself may not be a single species. These wild crabs run into many forms. In the northern Mississippi and prairie country are native apples good enough to be introduced into cultivation under varietal names. These are Pyrus Soulardii, a species bearing the name of J. G. Soulard, Illinois horticulturist. These crab-apples are probably natural hybrids between Pyrus Malus and the prairie crab, P. ioensis. Had there been no European apple to be introduced by colonists, it is probable that improved forms would have been evolved from the native species. In that event, North American pomology would have had a very different character.

There remains a very different class of apple-trees, grown only for ornament and usually known as "flowering apples." They are mostly native in China and Japan. They are small trees, or even almost bushes, with profuse handsome flowers and some of them with very ornamental little fruits. They have come to this country largely from Japan where they are grown for decoration, as the cherries of Japan are grown not for fruit but for their flowers, being of very different species from the cherries of Europe and America. The common apple itself yields varieties grown only for ornament, as one with variegated leaves, one with double flowers, and one with drooping branches. These are known mostly in Europe; but these forms do not compare in interest with the handsome species of the Far East.

All these differing species of the apple-tree multiply the interest and hold the attention in many countries. They make the apple-tree group one of the most widespread and adaptable of temperate-region trees. It will be seen that there are three families of them,--the Eurasian family, from which come the pomological apples; the North American family, which has yielded little cultivated material; the East-Asian family, abundant in highly ornamental kinds. There are no apple-trees native in the southern hemisphere.

The apple-tree, taken in its general sense, has a broad meaning. What may be accomplished by breeding and hybridizing is beyond imagination.

XI

THE VARIETIES OF APPLE

Every seedling of the pomological apples is a new variety. Some of these seedlings are so good that they are named and introduced into cultivation. They are grafted on other stocks, and become part of the great inheritance of desirable apples.

It is to be expected that in the long processes of time in many countries the number of varieties will accumulate to high numbers. No one knows all the kinds that have been named and propagated, but they run into many thousands. No one book contains them all, although some of the manuals are voluminous. Varieties drop out of existence, being no longer propagated; new varieties come in.

So the lists of varieties gradually change. A list of one hundred years ago would contain many names strange to us. Thus, of the sixty apples in "A Select List of Fruit-Trees" by Bernard M'Mahon, published in "The American Gardener's Calendar," in 1806, not more than six or eight would be understandable to a planter of the present day.

With the standardizing of practices in the commercial growing of fruits, the tendency is to reduce the number of varieties to small proportions; it is these varieties that the nurserymen propagate. Here and there over the country are still trees of the extra-quality but uncommercial varieties known to a former generation. If the amateur now wants to grow these varieties, he must find cions as best he can by patient correspondence, and graft them on his own trees. When I planted an orchard twenty-five years ago, I found cions of Jefferis here, of Dyer there, of Mother, Swaar and Chenango in other places.

In the enlarged edition of Downing's "Fruits and Fruit-Trees of America," 1872, are descriptions of 1856 varieties, of which 1099 are American in origin, 585 foreign, 172 of origin unknown. The lists are not only much smaller in these days, but the foreign element tends to pass out. With the introduction of the Russian apples for the cold North in the latter part of the past century, the importation of foreign varieties practically ceased, as it ceased also for the pears at an earlier date with the introductions of Manning, Wilder and others. The epoch of the "testing" of varieties passed away, and with it has gone an appreciative attitude toward fruits and even toward life that constitutes a sad lack in our day.

About thirty years ago (1892) I compiled an inventory of all the varieties of apple-trees sold in North America, as listed in the ninety-five nurserymen's catalogues that came to my hand. The inventory contains 878 varieties. In the present year, however, perhaps not more than 100 varieties are handled by nurserymen in Eastern United States. Probably the dealer and grower would consider even this small number much too great. The highly developed standardized business of the present day, aiming at quantity-production, naturally reduces the variety of products, whether in manufacturing or horticulture, and aims at uniformity. Under the influence of this leadership, we are losing many of the old products, varieties of apples among the rest.

Why do we need so many kinds of apples? Because there are so many folks. A person has a right to gratify his legitimate tastes. If he wants twenty or forty kinds of apples for his personal use, running from Early Harvest to Roxbury Russet, he should be accorded the privilege. Some place should be provided where he may obtain trees or cions. There is merit in variety itself. It provides more points of contact with life, and leads away from uniformity and monotony.

The leading varieties of apples, that have become dominant over wide regions, have been great benefactors to man. The original tree should be carefully preserved till the last, by historical or other societies; and then a monument should be placed at the spot. Monuments have been erected to the Baldwin, Northern Spy, McIntosh and other apples. We should never lose our touch with the origins of men, events, notable achievements, outstanding products of nature.

I fear it is now a habit with many fruit-growers to minimize the interest in varieties, placing the emphasis on tillage, spraying and management of plantations. Yet, the only reason why we expend all the labor is that we may grow a given kind of apple; the variety is the final purpose.

In this little book we cannot discuss varieties at length. There are special books on this fascinating subject. But we may have before us a compiled list by way of interesting suggestion. The list is sorted from the Catalogue of Fruits of the American Pomological Society, 1901, the last year in which the catalogue was published with quality rated on a scale of 10. On such a scale, Ben Davis ranks 4-5; Baldwin, 5-6; Wealthy and York Imperial, 6-7; Rhode Island Greening, 7-8; Northern Spy, 8-9; Yellow Newtown (Albermarle Pippin) 9-10. There is no apple in the entire catalogue of 324 kinds (not including crab-apples) rated wholly lower than 4 in quality except one alone and this is grown for cider only, although several varieties of minor importance bear the marks 3-4. Only two varieties are rated exclusively 10, the Garden Royal, a

Massachusetts summer-fall apple, little known to planters, and the familiar Esopus Spitzenberg. Of course judgments differ widely in these matters, as there are no inflexible criteria for the scoring of quality; yet this extensive list is probably our soundest approach to the subject.

The varieties in the catalogue of the American Pomological Society are starred if "known to succeed in a given district" and double-starred "if highly successful." North America is thrown into nineteen districts for the purposes of this catalogue (which comprises other fruits besides apples). For our purposes we may combine them into six more or less indefinite great regions: n. e., the northeastern part of the country, Delaware and Pennsylvania to eastern Canada; s. e., the parts south of this area and mostly east of the Mississippi; n. c., north central, from Kansas and Missouri north; s. w., Texas to Arizona; mt., the mountain states of the Rockies west to the Sierras, including of course much high plains country; pac., the Pacific slope, Washington to southern California.

Of the varieties starred and double-starred in these various geographical regions there are 107; these are listed herewith. Of course the intervening twenty years might change the rating of some of these apples, other varieties have come to the front, and certain ones of these older worthies are receding still further into the background; but the exhibit is suggestive none the less.

Arkansas--n.e., s.e., n.c., s.w., mt. Bailey (Sweet)--n.e., s.e., n.c., mt. Baker--n.e. Baldwin--n.e., s.e., n.c., mt., s.w., pac. Beach--s.e. Belle Bonne--n.e. Ben Davis--n.e., s.e., n.c., s.w., mt., pac. Bietigheimer--n.e., s.e., n.c., mt. Bledsoe--s.e. Blenheim--n.e., n.c. Blue Pearmain--n.e., s.e., n.c., mt. Bough, Sweet--n.e., s.e., n.c., mt. Bryan--s.e., mt. Buckingham--n.e., s.e., n.c. Canada Reinette--n.e., n.c., mt. Clayton--n.e., s.e., n.c., mt. Clyde--n.e., n.c. Cogswell--n.e. Cooper--n.e., s.e., n.c., mt. Cracking--s.e., n.c. Doyle--s.e. Early Pennock--n.e., s.e., n.c., mt. Esopus (Spitzenburg)--n.e., s.e., n.c., mt., pac. Ewalt--n.e., s.e., mt. Fallawater--n.e., s.e., n.c., mt. Fall Harvey--n.e., mt. Fall Jenneting--n.e., s.e., n.c., mt. Fall Orange--n.e., s.e., n.c. Fall Pippin--n.e., s.e., n.c., s.w., mt. Fanny--n.e., s.e., n.c., s.w. Farrar--s.e. Foundling--n.e. Gano--n.e., s.e., n.c., s.w., mt. Gilbert--s.e. Golding--n.e., s.e., n.c., mt. Gravenstein--n.e., s.e., n.c., mt., s.w., pac. Hagloe--n.e., s.e. Hoover--s.e., n.c., mt., pac. Hopewell--n.c. Horse--n.e., s.e., n.c. Hubbardston--n.e., s.e., n.c., s.w. Hunge--s.e. Huntsman--s.e., n.c., s.w., mt. Isham (Sweet)--n.c. Jacobs Sweet--n.e. Kent--n.e., s.e., n.c.

Kernodle--s.e. Lady Sweet--n.e., mt. Lankford--n.e., s.e. Lawver--n.e., s.e., n.c., mt. Lilly (of Kent)--n.e. Lowe--s.e. Lowell--n.e., s.e., n.c., mt. McAfee--n.e., s.e, mt. McCuller--s.e. McMahon--n.e., n.c., mt. Magog--n.e. Maverack--s.e. Milwaukee--n.c. Minister--n.e., s.e., n.c. Monmouth--s.e., n.c., mt. Newell--n.c. Nickajack--n.e., s.e., n.c., mt. Northern Spy--n.e., s.e., n.c., mt., pac. Northwestern (Greening)--n.e., n.c., mt. Oconee--n.e., s.e. Ohio Nonpareil--n.e., s.e. Ohio Pippin--n.e., s.e., n.c. Ortley--n.e., s.e., n.c., mt. Paragon--n.e., s.e., n.c., mt. Patten (Greening)--n.c. Pease--n.e. Peck (Pleasant)--n.e., s.e., n.c., mt. Peter--n.c. Pewaukee--n.e., s.e., n.c., mt. Porter--n.e., s.e., n.c., mt. Pumpkin Sweet--n.e., s.e., n.c. Quince--n.e., n.c. Ramsdell (Sweet)--n.e., s.e., n.c., mt. Red Astrachan--n.e., s.e., n.c., s.w., mt., pac. Rhode Island (Greening)--n.e., s.e., n.c., s.w., mt., pac. Ridge (Pippin)--n.e. Rolfe--n.e. Rome--n.e., s.e., n.c., s.w., mt. Stark--n.e., s.e., n.c., s.w., mt. Starkey--n.e., s.e. Stayman Winesap--n.e., s.e., n.c. Sterling--n.e., n.c. Summer King--n.e., s.e. Swaar--n.e., n.c., mt., pac. Taunton--s.e. Titovka--n.e., mt. Tompkins King--n.e., s.e., mt., pac. Twenty Ounce--n.e., s.e., s.w., mt. Utter--n.c. Vanhoy--n.e., s.e. Virginia Greening--s.e., mt. Washington (Strawberry)--n.e., s.e., mt. Watson--s.e. White Pippin--n.e., s.e., n.c., mt., pac. Wine--n.e., s.e., n.c., mt. Wistal--s.e., s.w. Wolf River--n.e., s.e., n.c., mt. Yellow Bellflower--n.e., s.e., s.w., mt., pac. Yellow Newtown--n.e., s.e., n.c., s.w., mt., pac. Yopp--s.e. York Imperial--n.e., s.e., n.c., s.w., mt.

There are many odd varieties of apple not found in any list but about which questions are likely to arise. One of these is the Sweet-and-Sour. There is an old ribbed variety of this name, the ribs having an acid flesh and the furrows sweetish; it is little known and of no special value. Apples are sometimes found that are sweetish on one side and sourish on the other. The reasons for this kind of variation are no more understood than are those responsible for variance in color or shape or durability. One yet sometimes hears the pleasant fable that sweet-and-sour apples are produced by splitting the bud when the tree was propagated.

The Surprise is a small whitish apple with light red flesh. It is indeed a surprise to bite into such an apple, but it has little merit. It is an early winter variety.

One is frequently asked about the Sheepnose apple, particularly by older people who remember it from early days and who deplore its infrequency in these latter times. The sheepnose shape--long-conical--is an infrequent variation, as apples go, and apparently none of these forms chances to have sufficient merit to keep it in the lists. The name is often applied to the Black Gilliflower, an old apple more than three inches long, dark red, of light weight perhaps because of the large core, ripening late in autumn to midwinter. It seems to be specially prized by children, perhaps in part because of its unusual shape and in part by its aromatic fragrance; but it is not a high-class apple, and is now little seen. With the Rambo, Vandevere, some of the russets, Early Harvest, Jersey Sweet and other old worthies, it probably will pass away unless rescued here and there by the amateur. To the lover of choice fruit nothing is old; every succeeding crop is as choice and new as is the new year itself, and one waits for it again and again.

One hears of seedless and no-core apples, as also of pears. The core is present but greatly reduced in size, and the seeds may be few and small. I have also raised practically seedless tomatoes. All these are infrequent variations that may be propagated by asexual parts (cuttings, cions), but as yet none of them has any outstanding value.

The reader will now ask me about the water-core apples, so much sought and prized by youngsters. The water-core is not characteristic of a variety, although occurring in some varieties more frequently than in others. It is a physiological condition, supposed to be associated with a relatively low transpiration (evaporation) so that excess water is held in the fruit. In certain seasons this condition is marked, and also in cloudy regions and often on young trees that have an over-supply of moisture. Yet such cores occur in old trees and sometimes with more or less regularity. What the physiological inability may be in such cases to dispose of excess moisture appears to be undetermined.

Now and then one finds a double apple, with two fruits grown solidly together, two blossom ends and a single stem. A seedling tree I knew as a boy bore such apples frequently, sometimes a score of them among the crop of the year. This, of course, is a malformation or teratological state. Apparently two flowers coalesce to form these fruits. On the tree of which I speak, the two fruits were about equal in size, making a large, widened, edible apple, but I have known of other cases in which a diminutive undeveloped fruit is attached to the side of a normal one.

Perhaps the oddest of them all is the "Bloomless apple." It is said to have no flowers. In fact, however, the flowers are present but they lack showy petals and are therefore not conspicuous. The bloomless apple is a monstrous state, the cause of which is unknown. Now and then a tree is reported. It was described at least as long ago as 1768, and in 1770 Muenchhausen called it Pyrus apetala (the petalless pyrus). The flowers have no stamens, and apparently they are pollinated from any other apples in the vicinity. In 1785, Moench described it as Pyrus dioica (the dioecious pyrus, sexes separated on different plants). The ovary is also malformed, having six or seven and sometimes probably more cells, and bearing ten to fifteen styles. The resulting fruit has a core character unknown in other apples but approached in certain apple-like fruits, as the medlar. The fruit has a hole or opening from the calyx (which is open) into the core; and the core is roughly double, one series above the other. The fruit, in such specimens as I have seen or read about, has no horticultural merit; but it is a curiosity of great botanical interest. It appears now and then in widely separated places, the trees probably having originated as chance seedlings. The fruits from the different originations are not always the same in size and form, but the flowers apparently all have the same malformed character.

The apple is preeminently the home fruit. It is not transitory. It spans every season. In an indifferent cellar I keep apples till apples come again. The apple stands up, keeps well on the table. Children may handle it. In color and form it satisfies any taste. Its rondure is perfect. The cavity is deep, graceful and well moulded, holding the good stem securely. The basin is a natural summit and termination of the curvatures, bringing all the lines together, finishing them in the ornaments of the remaining calyx. The fruit adapts itself to the hand. The fingers close pleasantly over it, fitting its figure. It has a solid feel. The flesh of a good apple is crisp, breaking, melting, coolly acid or mildly sweet. It has a fracture, as one bites it, possessed by no other fruit. One likes to feel the snap and break of it. There is a stability about it that satisfies; it holds its shape till the last bite. One likes to linger on an apple, to sit by a fireside to eat it, to munch it waiting on a log when there is no hurry, to have another apple with which to invite a friend.

Now I am not thinking of the Ben Davis apple or any of its kind. I do not want to be doomed to one variety of apple, or even to half a dozen kinds, and particularly I do not want a poor one. There are enough good apples, if we can get them. The days of the amateur fruit-growers seem to be passing. At least we do not hear much of them in society or in many of the meetings of horticulturists. There may be many reasons, but two are evident: we give the public indifferent fruits, and thereby neither educate the taste or stimulate the desire for more; we do not provide them places from which they can get plants of many of the choicest things. Yet on a good amateur interest in fruits depends, in the end, the real success of commercial fruit-growing. Just now we are trying to increase the consumption of apples, to lead the people to eat an apple a day: it cannot be accomplished by customary commercial methods. To eat an apple a day is a question of affections and emotions.

We have had great riches in our varieties of apples. It has been a vast resource to have a small home plantation of many good varieties, each perfect in its season. The great commercial apple-growing has been carried to high perfection of organization and care. More perfect apples are put on the market, in proportion to numbers, than ever before,--carefully grown and graded and handled. I have watched this American development with growing pride. The quantity-production makes for greater perfection of product, but it does not make for variety and human interest, nor for high-quality varieties. We shall still improve it. Masterful men will perfect organizations. The high character and attainment of the commanding fruit-growers, nurserymen and dealers are good augury for the future. But all this is not sufficient. Quantity-production will be an increasing source of wealth, but it cannot satisfy the soul.

The objects and productions of high intrinsic merit are preserved by the amateur. It is so in art and letters. It is necessarily so. A body of amateurs is an essential background to the development of science. The late Professor Pickering, renowned astronomer, encouraged the amateur societies of star-observers, and others. The amateurs in the background, disinterested and unselfish, support appropriations by legislatures for even abstruse public work. The amateur is the embodiment of the best in the common life, the conservator of aspirations, the fulfillment of democratic freedom. I hope pomology will not lag in this respect. In all lines I hope that professionalism will not subjugate the man who follows a subject for the love of it rather than for the gain of it or for the pride of it. In horticulture, when we lose the amateur, who, as the word means, is the lover, we lose the ideals.

Naturally, the nurseryman cannot grow trees of all the good apples that may be wanted. The experiment stations cannot maintain living museums of them, for their function is to investigate rather than to preserve. Arboretums are concerned with other activities. Is there not some person of means, desiring to do good to his successors, ready now to establish a fructicetum in perpetuum for the purpose of preserving a single tree of at least one hundred of the choicest apples, to the end that a record may be kept and that amateurs may be supplied with cions thereof?

XII

THE PLEASANT ART OF GRAFTING

If I procure cuttings of a good apple, what shall I do with them that they may give me of their fruitage?

The cuttings will probably be dormant twigs of the last season's growth. They may not be expected to grow when placed in the ground. They are therefore planted in another tree, becoming cions. The case is in no way different in principle from the propagating of the young tree in the nursery, of which we already have learned. The nurseryman works with a small stock, a mere slip of a seedling one or two years old. The grower would better not attempt the making of nursery trees. It is better for him to purchase regular nursery trees and to graft the cions on them; or he may put the cions in any older tree that is available.

I have spoken of my own collecting of certain dessert apples. I "worked" them on young Northern Spy trees, purchased when two or three years old; they were grafted after they had stood a year in the orchard. These Northern Spy trees, used in this case as stocks, were regularly grown by nurserymen. The Northern Spy was chosen because of its hardiness and straight, clean, erect growth, making it a vigorous and comely stock. Weak-growing varieties are usually rejected for this purpose. Some growers use Oldenburg as stock, and there are other good kinds.

From the young stock, the old head is to be removed and a new head (the new variety) grown in its stead. The tree, therefore, will be combined of three kinds of apple,--the root of unknown quality; the trunk or body under a varietal name; the top, of the variety desired. Any number of different kinds of apple wood may be worked into the tree if the tree is large enough. If the operations are well performed so that there are no imperfect unions, and if the pruning is judicious, the tree may be grafted many times, in whole or in part.

I have said that my father brought apple seeds from New England and that the resulting seedlings were top-grafted. One of these trees was early top-worked to "Holland Pippin," which seldom bore. It stood in the yard near the smoke-house, where it found abundant nourishment. It grew to great size. In time I became a grafter of trees for the neighborhood, and often as I returned at night would have cions of different kinds in my pockets. It became a pastime to graft these cions in the old tree. More than thirty varieties were placed there. It was with keen anticipation, as the years came, that I looked for the annual crop, to see what strange inhabitants would appear in the great tree-top. I do not remember how many of these varieties came into bearing before the tree was finally gathered to the wood-box, but they were a goodly number, probably more than a score. I used often to wonder how it was that the nutrients taken in by the roots of the Vermont seedling and transported in the tissues of the Holland Pippin, combined with the same air, could produce so many diverse apples and even pears (for I had pears in that tree) each with the marks and flavor proper to its kind. The little cions I grafted into the tree were soon lost in the overgrowth, and yet all the branches that came from them carried the genius of one single variety and of none other. And I often speculated whether there were any reflex action of these many varieties on the root, demanding a certain kind of service from it.

The cions (sometimes still called "grafts") are cut in winter or early spring, when well matured and perfectly dormant. Placed in sand in a cool cellar so they will not shrivel, they are kept until grafting time, which is early spring, usually before the leaves start on the stock. The cions may be placed on the tree by several methods, but only two are commonly employed,--the whip-graft and the cleft-graft. The former is adapted to small stocks, the size of one's finger or smaller; it is the method employed in root-grafting in the nursery, and Fig. 16 explains it.

The requirement is to cause the cion and stock to grow together solidly, making one piece of wood. The growing plastic region is associated with the cambium tissues underneath the bark. It is necessary, therefore, to bring the "line betwixt the wood and the bark" together in the two parts, and to hold the junction firm and also well protected from evaporation until union takes place. The method of putting the parts together, the form of whittling, is a matter of convenience and practice.

The case was put in this way by old Robert Sharrock, "Fellow of New-College," in his "History of the Propagation and Improvement of Vegetables by the concurrence of Art and Nature" (I quote from the second edition, Oxford, 1672): "Grafting is an Art of so placing the Cyon upon a stock, that the Sap may pass from the stock to the Cyon without Impediment." Batty Langley, in 1729, gave this direction in the "Pomona": "The Stocks being cleft, you must therefore cut the Cion in the Form of a Wedge, which must always be cut from a Bud, for the Reasons aforesaid; and then with a Grafting-Chizel open the Slit, and place the Cion therein, so that their Barks may be exactly even and smooth."

Still earlier (1626) did William Lawson, in "A New Orchard and Garden," set forth the rationale of the practice in his Chapter X, "On Grafting," in this wise: "Now are we come to the most curious point of our faculty: curious in conceit, but indeed as plaine and easie as the rest, when it is plainly shewne, which we commonly call Graffing, or (after some) Grafting. I cannot Etymoligize, nor shew the original of the word, except it come of graving and carving. But the thing or matter is: The reforming of the Fruit of one Tree with the fruit of another, by an artificial transplacing or transposing of a twig, bud or leafe, (commonly called a Graft) taken from one tree of the same, or some other kind, and placed or put to, or into another tree in due time and manner."

If the whip-graft is to be below the ground, it is sufficient to tie the parts tightly with string and cover with earth; if above ground, wax is applied over the string to prevent drying out. On the small shoots of young trees, the whip-graft is often employed, but it is not used in large trees.

The cleft-graft is shown in Fig. 18. The trunk or branch is cut off; two cions are inserted in a cleft made with a knife. The "stub" is covered with grafting-wax (Fig. 19). Cleft-grafting is the usual method for the orchardist.

In either kind of grafting, the cion carries about three leaf-buds. If "wood" (cion-shoots) is scarce, only one bud may be taken, but this reduces the chances of success. One bud may not grow, or the young shoot may be injured. The lowest bud is usually most likely to grow; it pushes through the wax.

In young trees set for the purpose of top-working, the trunk may be cut off at the desired height and two cions inserted. The entire top is then removed at once; this is allowable only on young trees. Probably the better practice is to graft the main small side limbs and the main trunk or leader higher up. Usually it is better to leave some of the branches on the tree, not removing them all till the second or third year.

In old apple-trees, the main branches are grafted, where they are an inch or two in diameter. Care is taken so to choose the branches that a well-shaped free-headed tree will result. Only a small part of the top is removed the first year, and three or four years may be required to change the top all over, the old branches being removed as the new ones grow. In about three years, or four, the grafts should begin to bear,--about as soon as strong three-year-old trees planted in the orchard.

Any variety of the pomological apples will grow on any other variety, but apples do not take well on other species, as does the pear. The pear may be made to grow on the apple, but the graft is short-lived and the practice is not recommended. Boys may graft indiscriminately for practice, but grown-ups, having arrived at the unfortunate age of discretion, must operate only on those kinds known to succeed when joined. I have never known a boy who did not want to graft anything, as soon as his attention was called to the operation. The boy does not take it for granted: he wants to try.

XIII

THE MENDING OF THE APPLE-TREE

Many accidents overtake the apple-tree. The hired man skins the tree with the harrow; fire runs through the dry grass; hard winters shatter the vitality, and parts of the tree die; borers enter; rabbits and mice gnaw the bark in winter; loads of fruit and burdens of ice crush the tree; wind storms play mischief; bad pruning leaves long stubs, and rot develops; cankers produce dead ragged wounds; fire-blight destroys the tissue; a poorly formed tree with bad crotches splits easily; grafts fail to take, and long dead ends are left; the tree is injured by pickers; vandals wreak their havoc. All these accidents must be met and the damages repaired. The surgeon must be summoned.

We must first understand how a wound heals on a tree. Note any wound,-- knot-hole on the trunk, place where wood has been removed. The exposed wound itself does not heal; it is covered and inclosed by tissue built out from the edges or periphery of the wound. This tissue is like a roll. It is the callus. Eventually the tissue meets in the center, and the lid is thereby put on the place, and it is sealed. The exposed wood has died, if it is the cross-section of a branch or a deep wound, and it remains under the callus a dead body. If the wood has not started to decay in the meantime, the place is safe, but too often invasion has begun before the process is complete, the rot disease finally extends to the heart of the tree, causing it to become hollow. If the center of the wound falls in, the callus cannot cover it, and an open sore remains. In these cavities birds may sometimes build.

Therefore there are two points for the surgeon to consider in respect to the wound itself--whether it is so placed on the tree that the callus forms readily; whether the wound is kept healthy during exposure.

All ragged tissue being removed, deep-wound surfaces should be kept aseptic. For ordinary cases, white-lead paint with plenty of linseed oil is a good protective from the germs of decay. On old wood, no longer active, creosote is good, perhaps followed by coal-tar. Usually, however, paint is quite sufficient. Small exposures usually receive no dressing. When the fresh surface wood is exposed by removal of bark, it is necessary to keep the tissue from drying out, and antiseptics are usually not applied. Bandaging with cloth is the usual practice, after the wound is cleaned and trimmed.

The repairs fall into two classes,--those that require merely removal of injured parts and treatment of the wounds, and those that demand the ingrafting of new wood.

We have learned, in the discussion of pruning, that long projecting ends of severed branches do not heal. The branches to be removed should be cut back close to the larger branch or to the juncture with another. In repairing injured trees, all projecting parts that do not have life in themselves must be removed. All wounds should be left smooth, without splinters or hanging bark. Decaying wood is to be removed, and the area cleaned out and disinfected.

The nature-lover may find much to interest him in the observation of knot-holes as he comes and goes. Every knot-hole has a history; this history usually can be traced by one whose eye is keen and who becomes practiced in connecting cause with final result. One prides oneself on the ability to work out the obscure cases. An old neglected apple orchard thereby affords much entertainment.

If a very large branch breaks off, the remaining part is cut back to fresh hard wood; antiseptic is applied; the other part of the tree may be shortened-in to aid in restoring the proportion or balance.

Deep cavities caused by rot are cleaned out, disinfected with bordeaux mixture, gas-tar, or other material, and the place filled completely with cement.

In some cases, new wood is added in the form of cions of last year's twigs. Such cions may be set around the edge of a stub, thrust between the bark and the wood, to start new branches where an important one was broken off. The cions are cut wedge-shape (much as those in Fig. 18) and a bandage is tied around the stub to hold them in place; the exposed parts are covered with grafting-wax. The operation is performed in spring.

Sometimes cions are used to bridge a girdle. Usually a girdle heals itself if the injury does not extend into the wood, and if it is bound up to prevent drying out; but when the injury is deep and the exposed wood has become dry and hard, the cions may be used. The cions are somewhat longer than the width of the girdle. The edges of the girdle are trimmed to fresh tight bark; cions are cut wedge-shape at either end; the ends are inserted underneath the bark at bottom and top of the wound; edges of the wound are securely bandaged; entire work is covered with wax. The cions are many, so close that they nearly touch. The buds on the cions are not allowed to produce branches. This process is known as bridge-grafting.

With some experience, the cultivator soon learns to make many deft applications of ingrafting. Sometimes a piece of bark may be used as a patch. In the bracing of crotches in young trees, the two trunks may be joined by uniting a small branch from either one, twisting them together to form a bridge like a bolt; they can be made to grow together, forming a solid union. Bolting the parts with iron rods, or holding them together by means of chains, is the usual and commonly the better method. The iron is not to go around a limb, however, for girdling results; the rods or chains should be secured by bolts bored through the wood and pulling against large heads or washers.

The usual repairs are easily made. When trees are badly injured, and particularly when the tree is low in vitality, it may not be worth while to engage in surgery. It may be better to plant a new tree. Saving very old trees by the mending processes is not likely to be satisfactory. The grower should transfer his affection to a young tree. If the tree has had good care throughout its life, it probably will not need much surgery in old age. The grower will be willing, when the time comes, to take a photograph for memory's sake and to let the tree come to a timely and artistic end.

XIV

CITIZENS OF THE APPLE-TREE

Many years ago, my old friend, the late Dr. J. A. Lintner, State Entomologist of New York, compiled a list of 356 insects that feed on the apple-tree. Later authorities place the number at nearly five hundred species. It must be a good plant that has such a host of denizens. The number of fungi is also large; and the tree often supports lichens, alg? and other forms of life.

The apple-tree is not single in its denizens. No plant lives alone. It has association with its fellows, perhaps contest for space and nourishment. It provides habitat for many organisms, many of which live on its bounty. I have never seen a bearing apple-tree that was not a colonizing place for other living things. We accept these things as matters of course, as being in place, living their part in nature. Therefore, one cannot understand the apple-tree unless one knows something of its citizenry.

Probably the most prominent citizen of the apple-tree is the codlin-moth. Its larva is the apple-worm, the one that makes "wormy apples," the burrows going to the core and out again. The insect is native in Europe, but has been known in North America nearly two hundred years, and is widespread in the apple countries of the world.

If one has screens in the apple cellar, one is likely to find small moths on them in the spring, larger than a clothes moth, about three-fourths inch in spread of the soft gray watered-silk wings. This is the imago or mature form of the insect known as the codlin-moth (it lives on codlins or apples). The larv?or "worms" were brought into the cellar in the apples; some of them crawled out, spun themselves in a cocoon and pupated; in due season the moth emerged, ready to lay the eggs for other larv? Ordinarily the fruit-grower does not see the moth, for it is a small object amidst the foliage of apple-trees; the larva or apple-worm he knows well.

There may be two or more broods of apple-worms, depending on the length of the season. In the northern apple regions of North America there is usually only one brood, with a partial second brood. The first brood is hatched from eggs laid by moths that emerge in spring. The moths come from larv?that have lain in cocoons all winter, hidden under bark on the trunks and main branches of the apple-tree, in crevices in nearby posts and fences, and sometimes in the ground. The pup?are the transformed larv?or worms that left the apple of the previous year, usually before it fell, and crawled down the tree to find a place to spin the silken brown cocoons in which they wrapped themselves to undergo the wonderful transformation.

So is the cycle complete: egg laid in early spring, mostly on the leaves; larva hatched in about one week, crawling to the young apple to feed, where it lives for perhaps a month; larva departed from the fruit to form a cocoon and to remain quiescent till it pupates the following spring (if there is no second brood) when it transforms into a moth; the moth alive for one week or ten days, laying perhaps as many as one hundred eggs or even more. If there is a second or third brood, the pupa resurrects in ten days or so into the moth; eggs are laid; larv?are hatched; pup?again are formed; and thus is the process continued. But the winter stage is the larva, although perhaps in store-houses the moths may emerge earlier and survive till spring.

The eggs of the first brood are commonly laid on the leaves and fruit. The young larva or worm eats very little on the foliage. It usually crawls into the blossom end of the apple. The young apple stands erect, with the calyx open (Fig. 6); later the calyx closes and protects the larva that hatched there, forming a good cover for its operations (Fig. 7). The worm drives for the core, where it eats the young seeds and burrows extensively; then, when nearly grown, it sets out for the surface, eating a straight burrow; an opening is made through the skin of the apple, but this exit is plugged until the animal is ready to leave the place and to crawl down the tree to pupate. The larv?of later broods may enter at the side of the apple, where a leaf affords protection or where two fruits come together; but the life-history is the same, varying in its rapidity.

This account discloses the vulnerable point in the life-history, if one is to destroy the insects and to grow fair fruit; if poison is lodged on the erect open-topped little apple, the young larva will get it before he injures the fruit. If the application of the poison is delayed until the calyx closes (Fig. 7), there will be small chance of reaching the worm. The best way to reach the second brood is to destroy all the first brood. The standard practice, therefore, is to spray the trees soon after the petals fall, with the idea of depositing arsenic in the blossom end.

But the season of egg-laying is long, often extending over a period of three or four weeks, for the moths do not all emerge from the cocoons simultaneously. It is customary, therefore, to spray again about two weeks after the first application, with the hope of catching the young worms on their way to the fruit.

There is no question about the efficacy of spraying. Its value has been demonstrated time and again. The methods and the materials may be learned from the experiment station publications in any State, wherein the advice is kept up-to-date.

In the days before the perfecting of the spraying processes, the codlin-moth was controlled by catching the pupating larv? Taking advantage of the habit of the worm to find lodgment under the bark on the trunk, it was the practice to scrape the loose bark from bole and large branches to destroy the hiding-places and then to tie a band of cloth around the trunk. Under this band the worms were taken, as they spun themselves up in the cocoons. This is a lesson taken from the industrious woodpeckers, who, in the winter, search the trees for the pup?and make holes through the flakes of bark to get them. The scraping of apple-trees is not much recommended now for the reason that this special necessity is passed, and because the better tillage and care together with the soaking of the branches and trunk in the spraying operation, tend to keep the tree vigorous and the bark properly exfoliated.

So the worm in the apple has a delicate and interesting history. From egg to imago the transformations proceed with regularity, and they are marvelous. Had we not traced the sequence, no man could tell by appearances that the larva, the pupa and the moth are one and the same animal. They seem to have nothing in common. So is the egg stage as different as the other three, but we are measurably prepared for this epoch, since we know seeds so well; the egg and the seed are analogous. That a moth in the air should come from a crawling worm in an apple is indeed one of the miracles of nature. The worm leaves the apple ere it falls; how the worm knows the time is again a mystery. By some instinct, it is able to cognize a dying apple. The later worms, either the lastlings from the early brood or the product of subsequent broods, may remain in the apple when it is harvested, particularly in an apple picked before it is quite mature and from which the worm has not escaped.

The apple-worm ruins the crop by killing many of the fruits and by blemishing the remainder. Seldom are there two worms in an apple. They seem to respect each other's hunting-ground. From the worm's point of view and from man's, one is enough.

If man has dominion and if he needs apples, then is he within his rights if he joins issue with the insects. Yet is the insect as interesting for all that. I think we should miss many of the satisfactions of life, and certainly some of the disciplines, if there were no insects. My apple-tree is a great place for a naturalist. Van Bruyssel wrote a book on "The Population of an Old Pear-Tree." "When certain blue spirits begin to flit about me," he writes, "I depart from my study to go and read, in what I am allowed, even by my clerical uncle, to call my book of devotions. The devotions I mean are not in my book-case. No publisher, if he ever thought of such a thing, could bring them out. They are a page of the book of Nature, opened in the country, under blue sky, displayed at all season." What a marvelous company Van Bruyssel found on his old pear tree; and what inexhaustible worlds did Fabre discover in the lives of the spider, the fly, the caterpillar, the wasps, the mason-bees and others!

Therefore we need not pause with the other four hundred and more insect citizens of the apple-tree. Some of them, as the San Jos?scale, are not peculiarly apple-tree insects. My tree has another crew of inhabitants, and to this company we may now have introduction.

The spots on the leaves and fruits are not deposits of dirt nor are they caused by mysterious conditions in the atmosphere, as once supposed, nor is it in the nature of leaves to be spotted and of fruits to be scabby; nor are the one-sided dwarfed fruits merely accidents. The organism responsible for these blemishes is less evident than the codlin-moth; yet what fruit-grower knows the eggs of the codlin-moth? But the organisms are as definite as are the insects; no longer are the fungi things without form and without positive cycles.

On the ground are apple leaves, shed in the autumn. On the leaves are spots or lesions,--injured or "diseased"--infected with the apple-scab fungus. Under a good microscope the investigator finds immature fruiting bodies in these areas. In the early days of Spring, these bodies or winter-spores mature. A rain discharges them in astonishing numbers. Rising in the air (for they are incredibly light), these spores lodge on the unfolding leaves and flowers of the apple, and there begin to germinate, invading the tissue. The tissue is penetrated and killed so rapidly that the practiced eye soon discovers a "spot." The leaf, if badly infected, may not reach full size; it may curl; it may die and fall; the tree thereby is injured.

From the fungus in the active diseased areas, another kind of spore develops rapidly. It is the summer-spore, which may be produced in prodigious numbers, and being discharged carries the disease elsewhere.

All summer the process of spore-formation and distribution keeps up. If conditions are favorable, the tree is invaded in foliage and fruit. The flower-stems in the unfolding buds are attacked by the winter-spores and the flower falls. The apples become spotted from the invasion of the summer-spores, perhaps misshapen. Late infections may not show at picking time, but develop on the fruit in storage. The affected leaves are cast in the autumn, the winter-spores begin to form, the snows come and hide the processes, in spring the spores mature; and so does the round of life go on and on.

There are beautiful forms in these fragile fungus threads that eat their way into the tissues of the host. There are fascinating phenomena in the growth and reproduction. Even so and for all that, man protects his tree by spraying it with poison, and thereby again does he have dominion.

The spraying for apple-scab is with lime-sulfur to which may be added arsenate of lead. This treatment, properly timed, may suffice also for the codlin-moth. As the fungus may attack the flower-stems and kill them, so is the first application made when the flower-buds open and the stems begin to separate, but before the flowers expand; the operator has a period of one to three days in which to spray. A second spraying is given just after the blossoms fall, as for codlin-moth; if the season is wet, a third application may be made ten to fourteen days later; if the fungus seems to spread, a fourth spraying may be applied in midsummer. These sprayings, variously modified, control not only the codlin-moth and the scab fungus but also scale, blister-mite, plant-lice, leaf-roller, case-bearer, bud-moth, red-bug and others.

In the tropics one sees trees bearing great burdens of orchids and bromeliads and ferns and mosses, and one wonders at the strange and exuberant population. Yet here is my apple-tree supporting epiphytes and parasites and insects, protector and nurse of a goodly company; and birds nest on the branches thereof.

XV

THE APPLE-TREE REGIONS

The northern hemisphere is the home of the apple, particularly Central Europe, Canada, the United States. In certain regions in the southern hemisphere the temperature and humidity are right for the good growing of apples, mostly in elevated areas. In New Zealand and parts of Australia, apple-growing is assuming large proportions. Their export trade to Europe and parts of South America has come to be important and undoubtedly is destined greatly to increase.

In Europe, where land is often limited and high in price, apple-trees may be planted closer than in America, even in field conditions, and more attention is given to pruning, heading-in, and the development of fruit-spurs in the interior of the tree-top. I noticed this practice in New Zealand, also. In these directions, the Europeans have much to teach us in the careful growing of good apples. In Europe, the definite training of the apple-tree begins in the nursery; quantity-production, with standardization, is not there the aim.

In North America the general practice is to let the tree take its course, reaching its full natural stature. The pruning is mostly corrective, to keep the tree in shape and to prevent the top from becoming too thick, rather than in the development of fruiting wood. The consequence is that our trees become very large, specially in New York and New England where they are long-lived. In the western country, as we have learned, the apple-tree tends to be shorter-lived and does not usually attain such great size. In the New York apple country, orchards may be in good bearing at forty to sixty years from planting, and individual trees may be productive much longer than this. The trees come into good bearing in ten to fifteen years. In the irrigated regions of the West, the trees may be expected to bear a good crop two to five years earlier; to what age they may attain, in large plantations, it is yet too early to state.

The commercial apple regions of North America are in Canada and the northern United States, comprising about two or three tiers of States, with important extensions southward into the mountains and in special parts. The Southern States are not known as apple-growing country, except in special restricted elevated areas, although there are considerable plantations near the Gulf of Mexico.

The geography of apple-growing on the North American continent cannot be better displayed than by copying the table of contents of the larger part of Chapters III and II in Folger and Thomson's excellent recent book, "The Commercial Apple Industry of North America:"

Commercial Apple Production in Canada

Nova Scotia Prince Edward Island and New Brunswick Quebec Ontario British Columbia.

Leading Apple Regions of the United States

Western New York Hudson Valley New England Baldwin belt The Champlain district New Jersey Delaware Shenandoah-Cumberland district Piedmont district of Virginia Minor regions in Pennsylvania, West Virginia and Virginia Mountain region of North Carolina Mountain region of Georgia Ohio Southern Ohio, Rome Beauty district Minor regions in Ohio Kentucky Michigan Illinois Southern Illinois early apple region Mississippi Valley region of Illinois Ozark region Missouri River region Arkansas Valley of Kansas Southeastern Illinois Colorado New Mexico Utah Montana Washington Yakima Valley Wenatchee North Central Washington district Spokane district Walla Walla district Oregon Hood River Valley Rogue River Valley Other apple districts in Oregon Idaho Payette district Boise Valley Twin Falls Lewiston section California Watsonville district Sebastopol apple district Yucaipa section Wisconsin Minnesota

The varieties of the South and the North, and largely also of the West and the East, are prevailingly different. Canada has a set of apples quite its own. These differences are marked when one visits exhibitions in the various regions. Let the visitor who is a good judge of apples in Michigan and Ohio attempt to judge them in an exhibition in the Annapolis Valley of Nova Scotia, in the Province of Quebec, in North Carolina, in Minnesota, in Oregon. He will be impressed with the wonderful diversity, as well as the undeveloped resources, of the continent.

Southward, apples do not keep well. There are no true winter apples in the Southern States, outside mountain regions. A winter apple of the North becomes a fall apple in the South. In fact, there are marked differences in keeping quality within a single State. On gravelly lands or warm slopes in the southern part of New York, the Northern Spy may become practically a late autumn apple; in the northern parts of the State it is a firm crisp all-winter keeper. In the winter apple, the ripening process proceeds in storage. When the season is so long that maturity is reached on the tree, the subsequent duration is relatively short.

It is not to be inferred, however, that apples are to be grown only in regions and soils naturally well adapted. Such adaptations should be controlling in commercial plantations; but if man has dominion he should be able to accomplish much in untoward or even in hostile conditions. Even the city lot may be able to yield a harvest, if the occupant of it is minded in fruits rather than in other things. Every observant traveler has noted cases in which good results in the rearing of plants and animals have been attained in places that no one would choose for the purpose: the man has overcome his obstacles. I was impressed with this fact in visiting a greenhouse in the Shetland Islands. Cultivation has been carried far beyond the optimum regions. The merit of the man's performance is measured in the excellence of his result rather than in the quantity of it. The application of skill is the highest test of ability in plant-growing, and this is often expressed in the most difficult places.

Whatever may be the adaptability of any general territory to the growing of apples in a large way, the probability is that a man of resources and skill will be able to raise good apples for himself, unless, of course, the region is prohibitive. The amateur may be a law unto himself in many of these matters, delighting in the ingenuity that enables him to overcome.

XVI

THE HARVEST OF THE APPLE-TREE

Finally the apple is ripe, a fair goodly object joyous in the sun, inviting to every sense. Hanging amidst its foliage, bending the twig with its weight, it is at once a pattern in good shape, perfect in configuration, in sheen beyond imitation, in fragrance the very affluence of all choice clean growth, its surface spread with a bloom often so delicate that the unsympathetic see it not; and yet the rains do not spoil it.

The apple must be picked. Do not let it fall. Probably it is over-ripe when it falls; the hold is loosened; its time is up. Wormy apples may fall before they are ripe; the worm injury, if it begins early, causes them to ripen prematurely. A premature apple is not a good apple, albeit the small boy relishes it but only because he may get his apple earlier; in the apple season, when ripe fruits are abundant, the boy does not choose the wormy one.

Pick the apple from the tree. It will do you good. It is ever so much better than to pick it from a box on the market or out of a quart-can in the ice-chest.

You will feel some sense of responsibility when you pick it, some reaction of relationship to its origin. We know that we understand folks better when we see them at home.

In varieties that mature before winter, the apple is of best quality when it ripens on the tree and is picked when fit to eat. In this respect it differs from the pear. One reason why store apples are usually poor is because they must be picked long before ripe to stand shipment. In my experience it is most difficult to find a man who will pick apples when ripe; he is usually possessed to pull them green, thinking that if the fruit is full grown and has a red cheek it is therefore ready to be plucked.

One would expect the best summer and fall apples to come from nearby local orchards, but practically this is not the case because the grower will not allow them to remain on the tree until they are fit. Of course the really ripe apple will not keep long and it does not stand rough handling, but this does not affect the fact that, for eating, an apple should be naturally ripe. In every city, small or large, a good trade can be built up for local ripe hand-picked fruit of the first quality, in competition with the best commercial supply.

Winter apples are picked in the Northern States in October, sometimes late in September. They are then full grown, but are hard and inedible. The red varieties are full colored; the green ones show more or less yellow. Light early frost does not injure them on the tree. Usually they are placed at first in piles or windrows; and from these piles they are barreled or boxed for market. If the choicest grades are to be made, they should be taken to a packing-house.

The apple is an easy fruit to pick. The stem parts readily from the spur or twig. Yet if the harvester is choice of his trees he will work deftly rather than roughly, not to injure the bearing wood. The fruits are placed in baskets as they are plucked, sometimes in a bag slung over the shoulders but this is not the best way when the apples are ripe. In the packing-house, the fruits are sorted into uniform grades if they are for market.

The better the trees are tilled, pruned and sprayed, the more uniform will be the crop, and particularly if the fruit is thinned on the tree; yet the second-class and even cull apples will be many under ordinary conditions. The purchaser, noting the price of extra-grade apples, may not realize that he buys only the remainder in a long process of grading, extending really over the season or even throughout the life of the orchard. In all this time, the grower has borne the risks of frosts and hail, insect and fungus invasions, lack of help, and disastrously low prices. A finished product of high quality is always expensive.

The usual apples on the open market are not the kind I have here tried to describe. They are the product of indifferent orchards or of careless handling. They are purchased for cooking; and the eating of apples out of hand because they are attractive and really good is an unknown experience with great numbers of our people. The polished shiny apples of the fruit-stands are a delusion. The practice of burnishing the fruits produces a most inartistic result, destroying the natural bloom and violating the appearance of a natural apple. It is one thing to clean a fruit if it is soiled (which is seldom the case with boxed or barreled apples); it is quite another thing to rub and furbish an apple as if it were a billiard ball or glass marble and not a living object that grew on a tree,--it sets false standards before the children. Yet all this is in line with much of our practice whereby, in cookery and manipulation, we disguise our foods and show our lack of appreciation of the products themselves.

For home use, winter apples may well be stored in boxes in a cool moist cellar if such a place is available. For best results in long keeping, the temperature should be maintained below 40 degrees F. In a cellar containing a furnace, the fruits shrivel from too much evaporation, as also in an attic or other dry room. If the fruit must be stored in such places, it is well to keep the box or barrel tightly closed, and the individual apples may be wrapped in thin paper.

The apples must be sorted now and then, to remove the decaying ones; if the fruit was carefully sprayed, handled and graded in the first place and not too ripe, the necessity of frequent sorting will be considerably reduced. But in any case, the keeping of apples, except under good cold-storage, is at best a process of continually saving the most durable fruits. An "outside cellar," if properly ventilated, usually is a good place in which to keep apples. With the use of furnaces for heating and the cramped quarters of city apartments, the keeping of apples for home supply is constantly more difficult.

There is no apple like the one that comes up fresh from the cellar on a winter night, cool, crisp, solid yet ready. It is the fruit of the home fireside. I often wonder whether one in a hundred of the people know what a really good and timely apple is.

The yield of an apple-tree depends on many factors,--age, size, thriftiness, care it has received, whether it has escaped frost and other injuries; and some varieties are much more prolific than others. Some apples are "shy bearers," and for this reason soon are lost to propagation unless they have some superlative merit; Yellow Bellflower is an example of a shy, or at least an irregular, bearer. The great commercial varieties are of course good bearers, as Baldwin, Ben Davis, Stayman, York Imperial, Oldenburg, Rome, McIntosh, Wealthy, Yellow Transparent, Jonathan.

An apple-tree at full bearing is a wonderful sight at the harvest, particularly in such varieties as McIntosh and Baldwin, in which the fruit is highly colored and hangs well toward the outside of the tree-top. While the first bearing year may yield only a half dozen fruits, the crop increases rapidly with the added years,--one peck, one bushel, five bushels, ten bushels, thirty bushels, even to sixty and seventy bushels on large sturdy old trees of some varieties. The amateur, however, first prizes the quality and regularity of his product for the sheer joy of it; then every added bushel is so much to the good.

XVII

THE APPRAISAL OF THE APPLE-TREE

Now, therefore, in these sixteen little chapters have I tried to explain what I feel about the apple-tree. It is a version to my friend, the reader, not a treatise.

As the interpretation is in the realm of the sensibilities, so do I aim not directly at concreteness. Yet as it is now the fashion to "score" all our products by a scale of "points," I make a reasonable concession to it. But I do not like the scoring of the fruit independently of the tree on which it grew as if the fruit were only a commodity. I know we cannot bring the tree to the exhibition-room, yet the perfect measure, nevertheless, is the tree and the fruit together. In these later times we have said much against the use of the museum specimen to the exclusion of the living object in its natural place: let us be cautious, then, that we do not forget apple-trees in our studies of apples.

Here I shall not arrange numerical scales of points for the apple-tree. Sufficient for this occasion is the naming of the points, letting the reader place his own percentage-value on each of them; for I am trying to teach, not to instruct.

Yet I must insert, for the reader's benefit, certain good rules and scores that have been adopted for the "judging" of the fruit by those experienced in these matters. This excellent exercise of judging fruits at exhibitions has gained much headway. Students of schools and colleges are trained for the "judging teams," and great technical perfection has been attained.

To be exact is an exigency of science. I fear that we make exactness an end, but that is neither here nor there on this occasion and I shall not now pursue the subject further; I hope the judging trains the judge to see what he looks at in other things as well as in apples, that it leads him into the pleasant paths of causes and effects, that it opens the eyes of the blind.

The customary judging of plants and animals and their products consists in assessing the attributes against a scale of perfection. Thus, if "form" or "conformation" is worth 10 points in the hundred (by the estimation of good authorities), the judge must decide whether the particular animal before him merits 6 or 7, more or less. So if "flavor" in an apple is considered to be worth 20 points of the hundred, the judge makes up his mind what rating, within that limit, he shall accord to the fruit he is testing. The arrangement in tabular form of the features for any product, with the number of points stated for each, all summing 100, constitutes a "score-card." Thus there may be a score-card for Merino sheep, another for Shropshires, one for apples, and for any other objects whatsoever.

At competitive exhibitions, the element of comparison comes in. Perhaps it is the only criterion to be considered in a particular case,--whether this apple is better than that or than any number of others, which of several "plates" or samples of apples merits first mention, which of two or more collections of varieties is altogether most worthy of a prize. In these cases, the different fruits or collections may be scored by the card, and the total footings determine where the award shall go. Or, the different entries may be judged in general, "by the eye;" this is the usual method, and is satisfactory in the hands of persons whose standing and experience carry conviction.

If one is to evaluate an apple-tree against a scale or code, these are some of the features, in relative order of importance, to be considered:

1. Whether the tree is typical of the variety, in shape, manner of growth, character of foliage and bloom.

2. Whether it is sound of all injury and disease, and free of blemish.

3. Whether it is duly vigorous and productive.

4. Whether its fruit is characteristic of the variety or kind.

5. Whether the pruning has been good; the thinning; the spraying.

6. Whether the performance of the tree has fulfilled reasonable expectations.

The judging of fruits is facilitated by such score-cards and explanations as the following:

1. For comparison of different dessert varieties.

Conformation 10 Size 5 Color 20 Core 5 Uniformity 5 Durability (keeping) 10 Condition 5 Freedom from blemish 10 Quality 30 ---- 100

2. For comparison of plates or samples of the same variety.

Form 15 Size 15 Color 25 Uniformity 25 Freedom from blemish 20 ---- 100

DIRECTIONS FOR JUDGING PLATES OF APPLES IN AN EXHIBITION

Following are directions and explanations issued to judging teams in exhibition contests, by an agricultural college:

(1) Form: The shape and conformation of the apples on any one plate should be typical for the variety, the region of growth being somewhat considered. All specimens on a plate should be uniform in shape. When competition is close, a careful comparison of the more minute characteristics of the basin, cavity and stem are made.

(2) Size: The specimens on any one plate should be uniform in size and of the size most acceptable on the market for the variety. A plate may be marked down for being either under or over the accepted commercial size. In many exhibits, the ideal size is given in the premium announcements.

(3) Colors: All specimens in an entry should be uniformly colored in the way that is considered perfect for the variety in the district where grown. In judging color, one should consider (a) the depth and attractiveness of the ground color, (b) the brightness and attractiveness of the over-color, (c) the amount of the over-color. In a yellow or green apple, the yellow or green should be clear and even all over, considering the maturity of the specimen. In varieties that are typically blushed, (e. g., Maiden Blush) the specimens should show a distinct tinge of red on the cheek exposed to the sun. With such apples as Rhode Island Greening, that are only sometimes blushed, the presence or absence of the blush should not detract except that the apples on any one plate should be uniform. With apples typically over-colored, an intense color for the variety is desirable.

The bloom may be wiped from apples, but in no case should polished specimens be given the preference. Some exhibits have special rules regarding polishing of apples.

(4) Conditions: Refers to the degree of ripeness. An apple to be in perfect condition should be firm for the variety and free from the withering that comes when apples are picked too green or when the fruit is over-ripe or has not been stored properly.

(5) Freedom from blemish: All specimens should be free from blemishes of all kinds. One should look particularly for (a) marks of fungous or other disease, including stippin, (b) injury from insects of all kinds, (c) mechanical injury, including loss of stem. Unmistakable evidence of codlin-moth injury or

San Jos?scale should disqualify a plate. Other blemishes are considered important in about the order named: Side worms, scab, stippin, curculio or red-bug, skin punctures, bruises, stem pulled, russet (not typical for variety) and limb rub. The extent of scab spots should be considered. Minute spots are not as serious as some other blemishes, while spots which deform the apple should disqualify the plate.

Other information: Five specimens constitute a plate, except when the rules of the contest or exhibit state otherwise. Any variation from this rule disqualifies the plate.

When a plate is not labelled with the correct variety name, it should not be judged, but is disqualified and if possible the correct name is applied. If one specimen on a plate is not as labelled, the whole plate is disqualified.

In some judging contests, the plates are not labelled with the variety name, and the contestant is supposed to make the identification.

Precaution: Avoid pressing the specimens with the thumb and finger so as to bruise the fruit. The degree of firmness can be determined by gentle pressure with the inside of the whole hand.

Defects, apparent or otherwise, should not be probed with the finger nail, pin, or other hard object.

Special care should be exercised to replace all specimens on the right plate.

Having in mind these definite criteria, the reader will know what is meant by a "good apple" and also a good apple-tree. Measurements of perfection aid us to estimate the deficiencies.

* * * * *

He who knows the apple-tree knows also its region. The landscape is his in every blessed year; he sees the chariots of the months come down from the distances and pass by him into the twilights. Clouds are his and the repeating shadows on the hills. The morning when the blossoms are laden with the fragrance of the night, high noon when the bees are busy, the gloaming when the birds drop into the boughs, these are his by divine right. The smell of new-plowed fields is his, with the urgent promise in them. Seed time and harvest, as old as the procreant earth and as new as the latest sunrise, are his to conjure. The verities are his for the asking, the strong things of cultivated fields and of wild places. And mastery is his, that comes of the amelioration of the land and the education of the tree. All these are everyman's, and yet they are his alone.

###